Praise for *The*

"D. B. Gilles' breezy, informal style makes the imposing task of writing a script seem manageable and even fun, and yet he slips in some pretty profound life observations that can give your scripts emotioal depth and weight."

— CHRISTOPHER VOGLER
author of *The Writer's Journey:
Mythic Structure for Storytellers and Screenwriters*

"*The Screenwriter Within* is the only book I know on the subject of writing screenplays that qualifies as a page-turner. It's Aristotle's *Poetics* as taught by Jerry Seinfeld."

— JAMES BOSLEY
Gotham Writer's Workshop (New York City)

"A sassy and first-rate guide to screenplay craftmanship. An attentive student of the writing game, D. B. Gilles stacks his deck with insights and tricks of the trade which are guaranteed to improve anyone's ability to tell a story well."

— DAVID MCKENNA
Columbia University Film Division

"D. B. Gilles has written a fresh, original tutorial. His lighthearted, humorous approach in tackling the intricacies of structuring a story will be of great value to any aspiring scriptwriter."

— FREDERIC LEBOW
screenwriter, *While You Were Sleeping*

"More than just the nuts and bolts of screenwriting. *The Screenwriter Within* is just like sitting in D. B.'s class . . . honest, practical and informative."

— SAL STABILE
writer-director, *Gravesend*

The Screenwriter Within

How to Turn the Movie

in Your Head into a

Salable Screenplay

D. B. Gilles

THREE RIVERS PRESS

NEW YORK

Published by Three Rivers Press,
New York, New York. Member of the Crown Publishing Group.

Random House, Inc. New York, Toronto, London, Sydney, Auckland
www.randomhouse.com

THREE RIVERS PRESS is a registered trademark and the Three Rivers Press colophon is a trademark of Random House, Inc.

Printed in the United States of America

Design by Donna Sinisgalli

Library of Congress Cataloging-in-Publication Data

Gilles, D. B.
The screenwriter within : how to turn the movie in your head into a salable screenplay / by D. B. Gilles.—1st pbk. ed.
p. cm.
Includes bibliographical references.
1. Motion picture authorship. 2. Television authorship. I. Title.
PN1996.G44 2000
808.2'3—dc21   99-046533
CIP

ISBN 0-609-80495-2

10 9 8 7 6 5 4 3

For

Jane Terese Campbell

CONTENTS

$\mathscr{P}art$ 1
STORYTELLING

Part 2
CHARACTERIZATION

Part 3

DIALOGUE AND CONFLICT

Part 4

FINDING YOUR NICHE

Part 5

SCREENWRITING TIPS
FOR LATE BLOOMERS

SPECIAL ACKNOWLEDGMENTS

Josephine Gilles, my mother, for encouraging me to take typing lessons in high school; Janet Neipris, mentor and friend; Sheldon Woodbury for consistently intelligent criticism; Jane Dystel, my literary agent, for her belief in the idea; PJ Dempsey, my editor, for her guidance and input; Don DeMaio for friendship and philosophical conversations; Margo Haas for friendship and belief since the early days. To my friends and colleagues at New York University: Venable Herndon, Mark Dickerman, Richard Wesley, Charlie Purpura, Paul Selig, Elizabeth Diggs, Len Jenkin, Gary Garrison, Martin Epstein, Gordon Farrell, Carol Rocamora, Fred Hudson, Leslie Lee, Viva Knight, Lonny Carter, Susan Dwyer, David Ranghelli, Wendy Kaplan, and Lamar Sanders. To the Monday Night Workshop, past and present, especially Lesley Starbuck, Robb Webb, Danny Ezell, Lorri Shundich, Caprice Crane, Gille Ann Rabbin, Elise Formicello, Alice Stitleman, Sharon Shapow, Lew Stallsworth, Ellen Maguire, and Brian Clark.

INTRODUCTION

𝒥n 1988 I walked into a classroom in the Dramatic Writing Program at New York University's Tisch School of the Arts and faced my first screenwriting class.

Having only minimal teaching experience and never having taught screenwriting, I was more than a little nervous. The chairperson of the Department, Janet Neipris, had hired me on a hunch, and I didn't want to disappoint her. My biggest fear was that none of the students would show up for the second class.

Fortunately they came back, and what I thought would be a one-time only teaching job turned into a new career during which teaching the craft of screenwriting became an integral part of my life.

I am a big believer in the concept "we don't know what we don't know." I also believe that we all have talents we don't know we have. Since that first screenwriting class in 1988, I discovered that there was a teacher within me waiting for the opportunity to break out. Over the years, I've been able to find my own voice, the result being a teaching style that is both irreverent and intensely personal, that explores how big-screen stories can come from the smaller events in our everyday lives—past and present. The keys are knowing where to look to find the best stories and how to blend fact with imagination and observation.

I think that there are two reasons people want to become screenwriters. You have a story to tell or a point you want to make. Maybe both. Some might take a crack at a screenplay because they've heard so many stories about million-dollar scripts, they figure, *Why not give it a shot?* But screenwriters with only this kind of motivation fall by the wayside fast. Writing a screenplay is just too difficult to be doing it only for the money.

The desire to write, to turn that movie in your head into a screenplay, must come first. This book will help you turn that desire into a reality.

I believe that screenwriting is a lesser form of war. We fight to find the right idea. We fight to develop it. We fight to create interesting characters. We fight to pound out a first draft to see what we have. We fight through subsequent drafts to get it as good as it can be. Then we fight to find an agent or a producer who will show interest. And of course all writers constantly fight with themselves just to keep on writing.

Although all this fighting might not make us soldiers, screenwriters do need a whole arsenal of weapons and strategies to write a good screenplay.

Teaching writing courses is much like teaching karate. The sensei will say that not only does the student learn from the teacher, but the teacher learns from the student. I can honestly say that I've learned from many of my students.

The more I teach, the better I become, not only as a teacher but as a screenwriter.

Most important, I've learned that we all have a story to tell. I know that the lessons I share in this book will help you tell yours and get acquainted with the screenwriter within you.

D. B. GILLES

NEW YORK UNIVERSITY

TISCH SCHOOL OF THE ARTS

HOW THE BOOK WORKS

The chapters in *The Screenwriter Within* are of varying length. They are as long or short as necessary to get the information across. Some make their point within two pages. Others take more. Some call for writing exercises, others do not.

Some of the thoughts I wanted to convey didn't merit their own chapters but needed to be mentioned and learned. To accommodate them, I've included 31 small but crucial tips. I call these little gems "Nuggets." They appear between chapters and collectively at the end of the book.

Most stand alone in their content. A few provide additional spin on a point previously mentioned. Think of the Nuggets as an easy reference/troubleshooting guide to turn to after you've finished reading the book and are ensconced in your screenplay.

" *Whatever* you can do,
or dream you can, begin it."

JOHANN WOLFGANG VON GOETHE

The
Screenwriter
Within

How 3 Punctuation Marks,
7 Words, and Basic Math
Serve as the Blueprint
of Your Screenplay

*"For the things we have to learn before we can do them, we
learn by doing them."*

ARISTOTLE

The most important idea you should retain from this book is the
Punctuation Theory of screenwriting.

ACT ONE ENDS WITH A ?

A man meets a woman who is married. (**Instigating Event—Words
1 & 2.**) But it's an unhappy marriage, so they begin a torrid love
affair. Will they get caught and, if so, will there be consequences? (**Major Dramatic Question—Words 3, 4 & 5.**)

Think of the Instigating Event as the thing that happens
that causes the rest of the story to happen.

Think of the Major Dramatic Question as the one thing
the audience wants to know.

ACT TWO ENDS WITH AN !

The man finds out the woman isn't married to an ordinary guy. Her
husband is a hit man for the mob who is incredibly jealous and

ruthless. (**New Information—Words 6 & 7.**) Will our hero run for his life or fight for her?

The New Information is the!

It is also the Turning Point for your hero. Because he loves the woman, he will most certainly fight for her, and this leads us into Act Three. Only now, the stakes have been raised.

ACT THREE ENDS WITH A .

The man must find a way to save not only the woman he loves but himself, as well as guaranteeing a safe future for them. In doing so his identity is discovered and the hit man is out for blood.

He wants both the hero and the woman dead. The hero finds a way to save them both and eliminate the hit man. He does so, and the two live happily ever after. Or he dies so that she may live. Or she dies so that *he* may live. But one way or another, the story has ended.

The Major Dramatic Question has been answered. Resolution. Fini. The story is over.

Unfortunately this simple thesis is surprisingly difficult to pull off, but once you understand its underlying wisdom, even before you start writing your screenplay you'll be at an advantage. More about this in chapters eight, 11, and 15.

DOING THE MATH

I failed algebra my freshman year of high school and geometry my sophomore year. Other than the embarrassment of flunking and the fact that I had to retake both classes during summer school, I remember not being all that worried. I assumed I would never have any use for either discipline in my life.

I was right. To this day, more than 30 years later, I have never utilized anything from those two classes.

I can add, subtract, multiply, and divide. I seldom find myself in situations where I have to "divide" anything, and multiplying isn't something I do that often. Subtraction and addition come in handy when I balance my checkbook or tally up a bill in a restaurant. It wasn't until I began teaching that the value of mathematics hit me.

There's an understanding in Hollywood that a screenplay has three acts and that most scripts come in at anywhere from 105 to 120 pages. Screenplays are broken down into three acts— although some break down scripts into five acts and others (typically movies for television) into seven acts. I prefer the three-act breakdown.

What is an "act"? By definition, an act is one of the principal divisions of a theatrical work, originating with plays and operas. As movies came long after plays and operas, it was only natural that screenplays were also separated into acts.

When I began teaching, I noticed that most of my students tended to have problems figuring out where the act breaks should fall. This is a problem for almost everyone, even people with a firm understanding of structure.

After reading dozens of screenplays of films that were made, I began to see a pattern. Act One tended to end anywhere from page 28 to 35. Act Two tended to end somewhere between 82 and 90, and Act Three was typically 25 to 30 pages. In the actual filmed version of most screenplays, timewise, the end of Act One usually came 30 to 40 minutes into it.

By utilizing the Punctuation Theory, it becomes easy to pinpoint where the act breaks should occur.

And by forcing yourself to remember that the ? should be presented between pages 28 and 35 (ideally page 30) and that the ! should fall between pages 82 and 90 (depending on the length of your script), you won't find yourself having a first act that ends too early (say, page 23) or comes too late (say, page 44).

A FEW MORE THOUGHTS ON MATH

Every screenplay-in-progress is filled with walls that every screenwriter either smashes into head-on or is blindsided by. Some are made of iron, some of granite, but most are sand. Wet sand. Lots of wet sand.

The first one usually comes around page 20. This is the place where many a new (and experienced) screenwriter is ready to throw in the towel on the project.

"I hate my idea" is the common excuse given.

"I have a new idea that's better" is another justification I hear over and over.

My response is always the same. "If you quit now, you'll hate your new idea on page 20 of that script and you'll want to start another idea, which you'll hate when you come to page 20 on it, and you'll spend weeks (or months) making false starts and winding up with 60 or 80 pages of abandoned scripts."

Unless a new screenwriter has tackled a monumentally complicated idea that requires more experience, I never encourage starting something fresh. Breaking through, climbing over, sneaking around, or digging under the page-20 wall is a rite of passage.

There is the periodic story about the screenwriter who churns out a high-six-figure script in eight days or three weeks or some maddeningly speedy time frame. But the fact is, 99 percent of screenplays aren't written fast, and I know enough screenwriters to back this up.

You should come to expect about three walls in your script. For me, page 20 is the most common, then around page 50, and then around the end of Act Two, which is somewhere in the '80s. And understand that there is great satisfaction in getting through them.

Giving up and starting a new script won't do much for your confidence. And as a new screenwriter, you'll need all the self-esteem and confidence you can get.

Nugget

Every Screenplay You Start Is Like a New Relationship

Screenwriting is like dating. You meet someone (**you get an idea**). Being with your new lover is so easy (**the first 15 pages almost write themselves**). Things look incredibly promising for the first four weeks (**Act One is done and Act Two is so well thought out, you can write it in your sleep**). Then all Hell breaks loose. You find out your new soul mate has a nasty little cocaine addiction/gives you an STD/is married/is a pre-op transsexual/doesn't really like children, dogs, cats, your friends, your hobbies (**the structure that seemed so right suddenly falls apart/your main character is boring/the dialogue is stilted/unfunny/dumb, and you have no third act and no ending and the most appealing character was killed off in the middle of Act Two**). When your relationship/ screenplay has hit a brick wall, you have two choices: End it, find someone new, and try again (**abandon it, find a new idea, and** start all over), or try to break down the wall by working through the problems (**try to break down the wall by working through the problems**). Unless you're in love with the person, end it (**unless you're in love with the idea, abandon it**). Because even when you're in love with someone (**or a script**), it's hard enough to make it work.

■ ■ ■ ■ ■ ■ ■
C H A P T E R   2

The Three *P*'s: Pivotal Plot Points

"With a tale, forsooth, he cometh unto you, with a tale that
holdeth children from play and old men from the chimney
corner."

SIR PHILIP SIDNEY

Drama is revelation.

Every few pages, something must happen to move the story along. This is what plotting is. Just as we plan the events of a special evening, we must plan our screenplays.

Whether you're writing an action/adventure that requires the proverbial thrill a minute or a gentle tale about two souls wounded by life who find each other, you must keep the story moving. And there must be dramatic tension.

Pivotal Plot Points are the key events that move the story forward. Think in terms of cause and effect. *This* happens, then *this* happens, then *this* happens. Every few pages, make sure *something* is happening.

If you've written a batch of pages (say five to 10) and nothing is happening (meaning the story isn't moving forward and we aren't learning anything important about the protagonist), this is a problem, even if your dialogue is brilliant and your stage directions sheer poetry.

Your protagonist must be talking about and/or doing things that are organic to the story or character development.

If all you've accomplished is to show us the minutiae of your protagonist's morning ritual from the ring of the alarm clock to how long she shampoos her hair to how thoroughly she flosses her teeth after breakfast, you've shown us (pardon my Zen) both too much and not enough. You will lose us.

If you want to spend time showing your main character preparing her breakfast, do so only if what she eats will make a statement about who she is. Whole wheat toast without butter and instant coffee with milk doesn't say much. But if you have her carefully trim the crust off the toast, then slice it into triangular pieces, then arrange them on a plate in the shape of a pentagram, then have her recite a witchlike chant in which she praises the god of wheatfields, *then* you've dramatized something important about her character.

Her breakfast ritual becomes a Pivotal Plot Point. And if your story has her meeting the man of her dreams on her way to work, the way she meets him becomes a Pivotal Plot Point. And as a result of meeting him, her daily routine is changed. She can't get him out of her mind. She tells a co-worker about the guy, and the co-worker encourages her to try to meet him again the next morning. This is another Pivotal Plot Point.

The next morning when we see her wake up, maybe she takes more time choosing an outfit, fixing her makeup, and combing her hair, all with the intention of bumping into the guy again, only this time the guy doesn't show. Another Pivotal Plot Point. She's bummed out. But she still can't get the guy out of her head. So from this point on all of her dramatic actions revolve around her desire to see him again. It's what she talks about. Now, she can talk about other things (her job, sick father, the brother she doesn't get along with, her interests—whatever), and through this dialogue we will learn more about her, but her primary behavior must be about meeting this guy again.

Once she meets him, you're on to the next set of Pivotal Plot Points revolving around whether he'll be interested in her and if they'll have a relationship. Once this happens, then it's just more . . . *this* happens, then *this* happens, then—well, you get the idea.

Nugget

People Don't Remember Plots

Other than film buffs and movie nuts, moviegoers don't remember the plots of most of the movies they see. People remember lines, scenes, and characters. Robert De Niro's "You talkin' to me?" scene in *Taxi Driver* is legend. But I'd bet a box of popcorn that 90 percent of the people who saw *and loved* the movie couldn't tell you the plot. Same with Clint Eastwood as Dirty Harry saying, "Go ahead. Make my day." Quick: Which Dirty Harry movie did he say it in and what was the plot? And Jack Nicholson's "You can't handle the truth" in *A Few Good Men*. What was the plot? And again, Jack Nicholson's diner scene in *Five Easy Pieces*. What was the plot? This is not to say that you should minimize the importance of plot and story. Those are a given. I'm simply saying that, save for diehard movie-lovers, film historians, and screenwriting teachers, plot tends to be forgotten while striking moments, lines, scenes, and characters live on.

Why Shakespeare, Sophocles, Aristophanes, and Other 2,300-Year-Old Greek Playwrights Would Be the Hottest Screenwriters in Hollywood Today

"The play's the thing."

WILLIAM SHAKESPEARE

The term *high concept* has permeated, if not dominated, mainstream Hollywood over the last 20 years. Simply, it's the catchy one- or two-sentence description of a screenplay's plot that encapsulates the story so succinctly that you can see the whole movie.

Blast From the Past (1999)

In the wake of the Cuban Missile Crisis, two paranoid scientists retreat to their underground bomb shelter to wait out the nuclear winter. They raise their son there for 35 years, until he ventures out into the world for the first time in 1999.

Analyze This (1999)

A mobster about to be promoted to Godfather experiences self-doubt and feelings of inadequacy, so he seeks counseling from a therapist who becomes his friend.

Stepmom (1998)

A divorced mother of two children discovers she is terminally ill and is forced to cope with her imminent death, deal with her ex-husband's engagement to a younger woman, and prepare her children for a future without her but with the wife-to-be as their new mother.

Jack Frost (1998)

A neglectful father dies and returns to life as a snowman, and in this new role tries to be the nurturing dad he never was to his young son.

Good Will Hunting (1997)

A troubled working-class kid employed in the maintenance department at M.I.T. turns out to be a math genius, and through the help of a sympathetic therapist the boy is able to fight his demons and pursue a new life.

Air Force One (1997)

The plane of the president of the United States is captured by terrorists, and the president himself must save the day.

Tootsie (1982)

An actor unable to find employment dons a dress, wig, and makeup, presents himself as an actress, and becomes a huge soap-opera star.

Now let's jump back a few years. Actually, a few *hundred* years.

Hamlet (1596)

A distraught prince talks to his father's ghost and solves his father's murder.

Romeo and Juliet (1598)

Two teenagers from families who don't get along fall in love and rather than be apart take their own lives.

Love's Labour's Lost (1599)

Three scholars give up the pursuit of romance in the quest for knowledge.

Oedipus Rex (Sophocles, 497 B.C.)

A man murders his father and marries his mother.

Lysistrata (Aristophanes, 450 B.C.)

An anti-war farce in which women deny their husbands sex until they stop fighting a war.

The Orestes Trilogy: Agamemnon, The Libation Bearers, and *The Eumenides* (Aeschylus, 525 B.C.)

A king, Agamemnon, returns home and is murdered by his faithless wife. His son, Orestes, avenges Agamemnon's murder by slaying his mother and her lover. Orestes is punished by the avenging goddesses, the Erinyes, who pursue him until he is cleansed of his blood guilt and set free.

There were other playwrights in ancient Greece, Rome, and Elizabethan England, but many of the plays that have stood the test of time and are studied in classrooms throughout the world are about topics that would fit right in now:

- incest
- rape
- ghosts
- insanity
- racism
- matricide

- patricide
- adultery

In short, all the dark, horrifying things men and women do that make life so treacherous.

Let's call a spade a spade: What works in Hollywood today worked in Athens, Rome, and Stratford-on-Avon way back when.

If there's a lesson to be learned from this, it's simply that the best stories seem to be about big issues, and the big issues, in one form or another, tend to deal with love, death, greed, power, envy, betrayal, and hatred.

For big issues to be dramatized, however, they need to be wrapped around a story that, by its very nature, makes an agent want to represent it, a producer want to buy it, and a studio want to make it.

Nugget

Drama Doesn't Have to Be Life and Death to Be Life and Death

There are different levels of drama. High drama literally concerns itself with death. Someone (a princess, a president, a good person) dies tragically, suddenly, violently, young. As human beings we regularly experience emotions that aren't nearly on the level of someone dying but are so "life and death" to our immediate peace of mind that we place tremendous energy and thought on getting them. The dream job, dream girl, dream guy, dream house, dream agent for your screenplay. Getting revenge, getting even, getting justice, getting *whatever* at the right price. In

Jingle All the Way, Arnold Schwarzenegger's desire to find a certain toy for his son was definitely life and death. Satisfying a craving. How many times in your life was your craving for a certain food so intense that you went out to get it even if it was the middle of the night or raining or snowing or—you get the idea. The point is, if you think you have to write serious dramas about big themes on life and death issues with larger-than-life characters, you're limiting yourself. It's the small things in our lives that obsess and consume us almost daily. Those are the "life and death" dramas that are universal.

What We Know Isn't Very Interesting, So We Have to Make Stuff Up

"No mask like open truth to cover lies, as to go naked is the best disguise."

WILLIAM CONGREVE

The first of my three wives was the daughter of a fortune-teller in a third-rate traveling carnival that set up its tents in my hometown in Alaska during the summer after my high-school graduation.

She was born in Trinidad and liked to boast that she was part Italian, part African, part American Indian, and the rest Haitian. Although she had only one eye, blue like Paul Newman's, which she covered with a black silk patch, she was gorgeous. She also enjoyed bragging about the fact that her father was a practitioner of voodoo and black magic.

Her name was Jullanja; she was nine years older than I and had been married two times before. Both of her husbands had died mysteriously after she had taken out life insurance policies on them. I didn't know that until three days after our wedding, when she asked me to sign a life insurance policy in the amount of $75,000.

I signed it for the same reason I married her. Because she asked me to. I had never had a girlfriend before, and here was this older woman, very attractive and sexy in a *Hee Haw* kind of trailer-trash way.

Anyway, I left my family with my new wife with the idea that I would become an integral part of the traveling carnival. Jullanja told me that the new guys always worked with the snakes, some of which were poisonous. She told me that her previous husbands worked with the snakes and that they made it through just fine.

So I started my apprenticeship with the carnival feeding, washing, and generally looking after 16 reptiles.

I became friendly with Omar, the snake charmer, and it was he who warned me that my wife was going to do to me what she'd done to her first two husbands, namely, kill me.

I didn't believe him. I was in love. And I was getting sex on a regular basis. And—

I made all of this up.

What really happened during the summer after I graduated from high school was so boring that I forgot it as I was living it. The only thing I remember happening was getting a bad sunburn.

In an era of comic-book movies, screenwriters have to put their imaginations into high gear.

Most screenwriters are couch potatoes. We'd rather watch movies or read screenplays or discuss movies and would be quite happy if we never had to leave our homes.

The days of the adventurer writer such as Jack London and Ernest Hemingway don't really apply to screenwriters. Most of the screenwriters I know either have degrees up the wazoo and never worked at anything more strenuous than being a stock boy at the Gap or maybe flipping burgers at McDonald's.

What we know and have lived is pretty ordinary and uneventful, so we have to plug in the imagination and make stuff up.

But while you're busy trying to come up with the fictions that will make up your story and main character, don't forget to continue to draw from your own experience as well as that which you observe.

What we know and what we observe should be the foundation of character. It's your capacity to be creative that will give you the idea for your screenplay.

Nugget

There's the Screenplay You Sell and the Screenplay That Gets Made

Before any producer or studio shells out cash for a script, somebody has to read it. Then somebody else. If you're lucky, only a few people will read it before a decision to represent or buy is reached. The point is, write a script that's fun to read. Make it a page-turner. Don't go crazy with long-winded, overwhelming stage directions. Don't make the people reading your script work too hard. Make sure your script hooks the reader from the first page. Set a tone quickly that says, "This is going to be a fun ride." Then make it one for the rest of the screenplay.

Things You've Forgotten, Denied, and Swept Under the Rug That Will Come in Handy Now

"Those who cannot remember the past are condemned to repeat it."

GEORGE SANTAYANA

Imagine that I'm sitting across from you and piled up behind me are several large suitcases and a couple of steamer trunks.

It's my history.

My baggage.

You have baggage too, but some of us have more because we're older and have been through more. That also means some people's baggage is probably more interesting—again because they've been through more.

You know what baggage is: the good, the bad, the ugly, the neurotic and all the weird little idiosyncrasies we come to know and deny about ourselves. With the passing of time, we also accept and understand them. Hopefully we've learned something from them. This allows us to create more fully developed, three-dimensional, nuanced characters.

The curse of youth is a tendency to see things in black and white. The ability to recognize shades of gray comes only with time.

I can't say this to the older people I've taught, those out of college ranging in age from their mid-twenties to late fifties. They have baggage as heavy as mine.

Some have more.

Some have baggage that's so bizarre I want to run screaming out of the classroom.

I once had the ex-wife of a notorious mobster in my Screenwriting Workshop. She was beautiful. Sexy. Smart. She was with him when he was assassinated. She saw him die one inch away from her. She'd been married to him for only three weeks. And her daughter by a previous marriage was there too.

Think her life was normal after that? What about her daughter?

Go ahead! Top that for baggage!

George Santayana's warning not to forget the past is meant to be a caution not to make the same mistakes again.

And again.

And again.

But another good reason to remember what happened to you is the gold mine of stories lurking, sometimes deep, within your subconscious. If you're going to be a screenwriter, you have to begin with a story, but where do you find the story you want to tell?

A good starting point is to look at the drama in your own life. It's there. Maybe not anything that happened yesterday or last week or five months ago or 10 years ago, but it's in your head or your heart or buried so deep inside that maybe you've forgotten about it.

Some of that drama didn't necessarily happen to you, but you might've been affected by it.

What I'm talking about are defining moments.

My first defining moment was the death of my father when I was 13.

I didn't know it at the time, but that was the beginning of my baggage. Specifically, my abandonment issue. Six months after my father died, my paternal grandfather died. And one month after that, my favorite uncle died. My issue with loss was in full gear, although I didn't know it yet.

I have other defining moments—some good, some bad: flunking out of college my freshman year, having a gun pointed at my head for 35 minutes during a robbery in my apartment, *surviving* having a gun pointed at my head for 35 minutes during a robbery in my apartment, deciding to remain in New York rather than relocate to Los Angeles, accepting a teaching position that was supposed to last one semester and having it turn into a life-altering career change, quitting smoking, buying a dog after being a lifelong animal-hater and transforming into an animal-lover.

I have plenty more baggage too.

So do you.

So does everybody, with time. That's why dating becomes so much more complicated as you get older. When a 15-year-old boy asks out a 14-year-old girl and it's her first date and he's maybe gone out with two other girls, when they sit down to talk there's not a lot of history.

But tag on 20 years to the same two and throw in a divorce, children, a drinking problem, depression, a business that failed, money problems, loss of hair, an addiction to pornography and—you get the idea. Both of them will have a lot more "stuff" to work around and/or hide.

Most people are afraid to confront their baggage, let alone talk about it.

Writers not only have to drag their baggage out of the closet, but we have to relive it and analyze it and take it out to dinner. And if we're lucky, maybe we'll find the first nugget of an idea in our quest for a story.

Grab a pen and notebook. Take a journey into your past and write down five of your defining moments, the good and the bad—preferably the bad.

Why?

YOUR MOST INTERESTING EXPERIENCES ARE THE ONES YOU'D LIKE TO FORGET

Interesting from a dramatic point of view.

People are more interested in hearing me tell what it was like to have a gun pointed at my head for 35 minutes than the day I quit smoking. I consider quitting smoking one of the genuine achievements of my life, but an exciting tale it isn't.

Think about it. What's more dramatic to talk about? That horrible day off the coast of Peru when you narrowly escaped being eaten by a hammerhead shark by killing it with your bare hands or the day you found out you got that scholarship?

Both events are linchpins in your life, but only one is the kind of story you'd share around a campfire.

As for that list of defining moments, after you've written them down, study them. Place them in their order of importance. Then try to remember how you felt when you were experiencing them. Maybe, just maybe, you'll find a launch pad for a story.

Nugget

Immediacy

Don't take too long to get the story started. Just try to have your Instigating Event happen as soon as possible. Page one is great. So is page two or three. Four isn't bad either. You know where I'm going with this. If you're on page nine or 10 and you're still setting things up, you're heading for trouble.

CHAPTER 6

Everything That Can Go Wrong
Must Go Wrong (Murphy's *Other* Law)

"Shit happens."

ANONYMOUS

Things can't go too smoothly for your main character. He has to want something, but before he gets it (*if* he gets it) he has to go through Hell or at least suffer a lot. Not a little. A lot!

Otherwise it's boring.

It's no fun watching somebody get what he wants too easily. What hooks us is when we feel empathy with the hero. We like him. We want him to be happy. We identify with him. We *become* him.

But no matter how much we like him, if he doesn't suffer enough, we're going to turn on him. It's like in life. If a guy is born with good looks, brains, money, charm, athletic prowess, gets all the girls, is popular with men, goes to the right schools, marries into the right family, has the right connections, slides easily into a great job and seems, on the surface at least, to just sail through life, it's not interesting.

In movies, nobody roots for the rich kid. It's the underdog that people always root for—the kid from the wrong side of the tracks with the alcoholic dad and depressed mom, with zero connections and nothing but a kind heart and good soul. It's fun to watch him struggle to the top. It's no fun watching the good-looking rich kid struggle to the top because he was born there.

However—there *is* a way to make the rich kid a sympathetic character. Give him parents who don't love him. Make him an only child surrounded by possessions but no love or attention except from the maid, who makes him peanut-butter sandwiches when the chauffeur drives him home to an empty mansion. And give him a complex about friendship. He's convinced the only reason people like him is because he has money. And give him a stutter that makes him self-conscious. If you really want to win people over, give him a dark secret: He was molested by the guy who cleans the pool.

Suddenly the rich kid has a nifty set of baggage and we feel sorry for him instead of being ambivalent about him.

He won't have the same set of obstacles and complications as the poor kid, but we'll at least be able to put aside the fact that he has money and feel sorry for him because of the negative things getting in his way.

One of my students wrote a script about a nuclear bomb dropping on Manhattan. Main character was a cop, estranged from his wife and young son. In the course of the story, the bad guy kidnaps the cop's wife and son, so the cop's primary action is to find them. Finally, lo and behold, he finds them, he and his wife realize they love each other, and the family is back together.

Then the bomb drops. And the cop is again separated from his wife and child.

End of Act Two. New Information. The Exclamation Point !

It was a really nifty touch. Guy wants something, gets it, then loses it and has to get it back, only now, because of the reconciliation, it's even *more* important to him that he finds them.

Here was the problem: The student's third act was only 11 pages long.

Despite his excellent ! at the end of Act Two, his choices for Act Three were disastrous.

First of all, he had the cop find his wife on the next page. Then he had them find their son two pages later. The remaining eight pages of the script had the three of them wandering around looking for a safe place to hide.

Boring.

As I told the writer, to draw us into his story, the cop had to go through one trial after another before finding his family. And he would have to decide who he would have to find first. Probably take 10 pages to locate the wife, one or two pages before the end of the script, another 10 locating the son, and he would have to be at great personal risk as he did so.

Once the kid is safe and sound and he reunites with his wife, it's over. But give it 30 pages, not 11.

The best movies to study for exciting third acts filled with complication after complication are action films, and the best example of a state-of-the-art action flick is *Die Hard*. Bruce Willis is a cop who fights terrorists single-handedly. His wife is one of the hostages, and he knows the terrorists are really bad guys, and he loves his wife, but they've had problems, but they were going to try and reconcile, and he's willing to die for her, so he goes through Hell to save her and the other hostages, and along the way there's some laughs and dramatic tension and thrills—and it works.

So by the time it's over, he's gotten what he wants and we've gotten what we want—a couple of hours of escapist fun.

Same with a smaller, softer movie.

Call them what you will—complications, obstacles, road-blocks, walls—the more your character has to deal with, the better your script will be.

Nugget

Sometimes the Structure Finds Itself

You've plotted out a solid three-act storyline. You've begun writing the screenplay, and things are rolling along smoothly just as you planned. But then you find yourself on page 19, which in your well-planned scenario was supposed to be the end of Act One on page 30. You have two choices: (A) Find a new event to be the end of Act One or (B) Pad those 19 pages up so they'll stretch out to page 30. Trust me on this: Padding is easier said than done. Better to let the chips, as they say, fall where they may. Keep writing. Trust the writing. Trust your subconscious to open a new door to go through. This can also happen when you're in Act Two and Act Three territory. Just as the best-laid plans of mice and men often go astray, so does the most well prepared, thought out structure. If you've gone through two or three unexpected doors, see where they take you.

The Screenwriter as Jock

"How do you get to Carnegie Hall?"
"Practice."

OLD JOKE

Once the star high-school quarterback wins his scholarship to Notre Dame, he keeps practicing and learning from his coaches.

And once he becomes the star college quarterback who receives national prominence and gets drafted into the pros for $15 million, he keeps practicing and learning from his coaches.

And once he becomes a star professional quarterback, he keeps practicing and learning from his coaches, as well as from all his experience.

And until the morning of the last game he plays in his professional career, he keeps practicing.

Screenwriters have to "practice" in much the same way. We have to keep writing, and when we're not writing we have to be thinking things through: plot points, character motivation, dramatic peaks and valleys, act breaks, which scenes to cut, which scenes to embellish, making sure the story has a logical flow.

Just as the professional quarterback keeps working at perfecting his moves, keeping his arm free from cramps, making sure his timing is on, continually going over old plays and new plays, and studying films of his opponents, screenwriters must constantly be examining and dissecting their ideas. What often makes perfect sense in your head or while you're writing it totally falls apart when you see it as part of the whole.

And just as every new game presents different problems and obstacles for that quarterback, every new idea, outline, treatment, and screenplay present new problems for the screenwriter. Not just for a screenwriter finishing a first script, but for all screenwriters, 10, 20, and 30 years into a career.

If you can't relate to sports analogies, think of the screenwriting process as dating. Every new person you go out with is different, and every relationship has its own set of unique problems.

Screenwriters go through the same process. You get that vague idea, stretch it into a premise, then pound out the three-act breakdown.

Then you write it, all the while dodging bullets and things that don't make sense and bouncing ideas off friends and getting feedback and plowing forward until you finish the first draft.

Then start all over and do it again and again and again until you get it right.

Then you start the next one.

Nugget

Keep Us Guessing

Fool me until I'm on the last page of your screenplay, and you've done your job as a screenwriter. I know how most screenplays and movies are going to end simply because I see things coming. My guess is that a lot of moviegoers of all ages are like this too. Character behavior and plots that are predictable quickly become boring. All the fun is taken away and you start to regret dishing out that ever-increasing price of admission. People love being fooled and surprised when things go unexpectedly in a different direction. This is even more important in a screenplay. You overcome a gigantic hurdle by keeping agents, producers, and development executives guessing until the final fade-out.

If Aristotle Were Alive Today, He'd Be Running a Hollywood Studio

"The beginning is the most important part of the work."

PLATO

Aristotle lived more than 2,300 years ago, but the ideas and theories on storytelling he set down in his *Poetics* are more timely than ever. If he were alive today, Aristotle would be quite capable of running a Hollywood studio, and he would have hard, fast rules that the screenwriters working for him would have to live by.

The six most important words Aristotle, wearing sandals and a toga, might have said to storytellers in Athens are the same six words he would say to screenwriters in Hollywood today as he sat in his stretch limo clad in Armani, sipping Evian, and making reservations at Spago: "Story, story, and story." Followed by "Character, character, and character."

If you never read the *Poetics,* or if you haven't read them since college, it might be worth another look. But having lectured on the *Poetics* for years I've drawn two conclusions:

1. Brilliant as he was, Aristotle tended to overwrite and get incredibly pedantic (or perhaps the blame should go to the translators). For this reason, poring through the 40-some-odd pages isn't an easy read.

2. But if you get through it, you come away with three important rules that can never be ignored.

RULE 1
STORY IS EVERYTHING

The most interesting characters "just talking" are not compelling for very long. Think of the guy who tries to tell you about the funny thing that happened on his vacation, but he rambles on and on, going off on tangents, never getting to the point.

He's lost you. And screenplays without a story, however slight, will lose the people reading them. (Understand now that it's the people reading your screenplay that matter more than any audience because *somebody*—an agent, producer, investor, creative executive, development person—must read your script before anything can happen. The object is to get the person not to put the manuscript down after 15 pages or even less.)

Something must happen to the hero that propels him on a different course, either by his own doing or because something has been done to him.

HIS OWN DOING

He knowingly or intentionally commits an act that will have repercussions if found out. He commits a crime, cheats on his wife, drives drunk, flirts with his boss's wife, bets the mortgage money on a horse race.

SOMETHING DONE TO HIM

He is the innocent victim of someone else's actions. His wife is murdered and he's accused, he's unjustifiably fired, while on vacation his teenage daughter is kidnapped.

RULE 2
THE STORY MUST START AT THE RIGHT TIME

Specifically, not too late. The earlier the better. Don't take 40 pages to establish who your character is and what the situation she finds herself in will be. In a novel and, to a lesser extent, a play, you can ease into plot and character. In a screenplay you can't.

RULE 3
KEEP THE LINE OF
DRAMATIC ACTION MOVING

This is where plot and complications come in. Plot is the placement of dramatic incidents. This happens, then that happens, then this, then that, then—

Complications are the things that get in the hero's way. They shouldn't be insurmountable, but don't make them a breeze to overcome.

It's like dating. You're a guy waiting in line at a bank. The woman in front of you is attractive. You might say, "Hi. You're cute. I love you. Want to get married?" And she might say, "Okay. There's a justice of the peace around the corner. Let's go."

The story's over. It lasted barely 10 seconds. There was no challenge for the hero and nothing compelling for the audience to care about or root for or root against.

But if the situation were more realistic—

Same guy, same woman, same line, same bank.

The guy starts up a conversation. The woman ignores him. He persists. She tells him to buzz off. He tries one more time. This time she's had it and says, "I could never go out with you because you look like the man I hate most in the world."

Now we have a story.

Turns out the guy loves a challenge (which in itself is a good character attribute), so despite the woman's honesty, he will attempt to overcome all obstacles and win her heart. And to really make it interesting, after he finally does win her undying devotion, then he doesn't want her. Now she wants him.

And to make it even more compelling, she's psychotic and has a history of tormenting men who reject her.

And to make this script even more of a page-turner, the guy has an "issue" about being pursued by women, so the harder she chases him, the more he's turned off.

By the time all these twists and turns have occurred, we like these people. Both are damaged, and because we've spent 100 pages with them, we've come to care about them despite their foibles and neuroses. We just know they'd be perfect for each other (with some couples therapy), so as we read the final pages, we're sincerely hoping they get together.

And on the last page of the script, they do.

And we're satisfied.

That's a story.

Nugget

Length

Length is a major problem for all screenwriters. You're either an overwriter or underwriter. I'm not talking about people who finish scripts that come in at 168 pages (way too long) or 83 pages (way too short). I mean scripts that should be cut or embellished by only a few pages. There is a trick that helps. If your agent tells you to get your 126-page script down to 119, and if you use *cut-to*'s, eliminate them. On the other hand, if your agent says to bulk up your 98-page script and you *didn't* use *cut-to*'s, use them. Don't think of this as cheating or padding. It's simply a way to make your life easier.

How Big Is Your Idea?

"Size doesn't matter."

COMMON FEMALE REFRAIN

"Size does matter."

COMMON MALE BELIEF

Prose writers go through this all the time. Is the idea a short story, novella, short novel, or full-blown novel? Playwrights must decide whether their new idea is a 10-minute play, short one-act (15 to 30 pages), long one-act (30 to 60 pages), or full-length two- or three-act play.

Screenwriters are in the same boat, and it's a less flexible boat. Is it a short screenplay or full length? And unless you're a film student in a class where your assignment is to make a short film (usually anywhere from five to 30 minutes), there isn't much of a call for short scripts like these.

The only other reason to write a short screenplay is if you plan to direct and produce it as a showcase for yourself. The fact is that most new screenwriters, although the possibility of directing looms as something for the future, are mainly concerned with writing a full-length screenplay.

This is where you must make important decisions.

Is your idea big enough to sustain interest for 115 pages? What do I mean by "big enough"? Consider the various movies inspired by sketches that originated on *Saturday Night Live*. Most didn't work, didn't get good reviews, and didn't make money. The reason being that what is hilarious in seven-minute bits seen a dozen times over two or three seasons is difficult to translate into a long-form storyline that is as consistently funny as the sketches.

"Less is more" clearly applies. Not that all the *Saturday Night Live* spinoffs didn't work. *Wayne's World* did. At least the first one. *A Night at the Roxbury* was entertaining although it petered out near the end. *Coneheads* seemed like a natural, but it too somehow just seemed to drag on. As a huge fan of Chris Farley, I felt the first three movies he made were fun (*Tommy Boy*, *Black Sheep*, and *Beverly Hills Ninja*), essentially playing off his good-natured/big kid/slob persona.

The best way to gauge what length your script should be is to use the song test. Most pop songs come in around three minutes. But some of the greatest rock songs ever recorded are unusually short or unusually long. "MacArthur Park" by Jimmy Webb, "Hey Jude" by John Lennon and Paul McCartney, and Don McLean's "American Pie" were each over five minutes. Dylan's "Like a Rolling Stone" was the first to break the three-minute taboo, and it worked not only because it was a great song, but it was a song that needed to be that long.

But Joe Cocker's hit "You Are So Beautiful" was barely two minutes. And Lennon and McCartney's "I Will" was well under three minutes.

All things being equal, if you have a hunch that your idea isn't big enough or if you start working on it and your gut feeling is that it's not sustainable for a hundred pages, you have two options: Find a strong subplot or have the courage to junk the idea until you *can* find a subplot.

Nugget

Bad Boys and Dangerous Women

What is the appeal of the so-called bad boy to a sensible woman who should know that he's going to break her heart sooner or later? It's the same peculiar thing that makes guys with their heads screwed on straight lose all sense of reason and fall for the chick who likes to dance on tables in bars, flirt with other guys in his presence, and have sex in public. Check out Jeff Daniels and Melanie Griffith in *Something Wild,* Sandra Bullock and Ben Affleck in *Forces of Nature,* and Warren Beatty and Goldie Hawn in *Shampoo*.

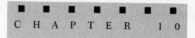

CHAPTER 10

Before You Can See the World, You Have to Get to the Airport

"Who so neglects learning in his youth loses the past and is dead for the future."

EURIPIDES

Drunk frat boys notwithstanding, it's fair to assume that most people don't just decide on pure whim to drop what they're doing, jump in the car, and take a 3,000-mile cross-country trip.

If we're going to take a trip or vacation, we usually have some semblance of a plan. We're going to drive from New York to Los Angeles and along the way stop in Pittsburg, Kansas, to visit Aunt Grace, then we're going to make a quick visit to Yellowstone National Park, and if there's time we're stopping in Phoenix to see Uncle Hank.

That's the plan. You know where you're going. You've given yourself an estimated time frame, budgeted your money, and—if you're really responsible—made motel reservations.

Structuring a plot should be handled in the same way.

It isn't wise to just sit down and start writing without even the remotest thread of a plot. Even the barest semblance of a plan will help.

In the world of television, they call it the Logline, usually a catchy sentence describing the episode of a particular show: "In this week's episode of *Frasier*, Frasier begins dating a graduate student who is putting herself through school by stripping, a fact that awakens his caretaking tendencies." It's clear enough to give us an idea of the nature of the episode.

Think of this sentence as

THE VAGUE IDEA

The Vague Idea is the slim notion of a story that tweaks your imagination. The following examples are from Steven Spielberg movies: *Jaws, E.T.,* and *Saving Private Ryan,* plus one original created by me, titled *Little Helpers.*

- A great white shark terrorizes a town.
- An alien child is left behind on Earth and must find a way to get home.
- After surviving the brutal D-day invasion, eight American soldiers must go behind enemy lines to find a GI and bring him back safely.
- An elf is denied employment by Santa Claus because he's too tall.

Next comes the expansion of the Vague Idea into a

BASIC PREMISE

This might be only a few sentences that help to clarify where the story might go. Remember, you haven't written a word of the script yet. You're just thinking at this point.

EXPANSION OF THE VAGUE IDEA OF *JAWS* INTO A BASIC PREMISE

A great white shark terrorizes a *beach* town during the *lucrative Fourth of July weekend.* (**Suddenly the stakes are raised. If the**

town, which relies on summer tourist trade, lets it be known that a great white shark is in the water, the town and small businesses risk financial ruin.) More expansion: Two people are killed. A shark expert is called in who says the predator isn't just a shark but a great white! The beaches must be closed, but the town and local businesses still have to worry about financial ruin, so an eccentric local fisherman is hired to find and kill the great white. Helping him is the local sheriff and the shark expert. In the course of the story, the three form an odd bond and eventually kill the shark.

This expansion tells us more about the story. The next step is to expand it into a three-act storyline. This is the hard part, especially for new writers. It forces you to think your idea through to the point where it's no longer an idea, but a larger premise and fuller concept.

Here's an exercise to force yourself to think beyond the Vague Idea, through the Basic Premise, and into a fairly thought-out storyline.

A guy meets this girl and they get together. (Way too vague.)

A guy meets this girl he used to know. (Not much better.)

A guy meets this girl he used to know in high school who played a hurtful prank on him with her girlfriends that made him mistrustful of women. (Getting closer.)

Let's pump up the volume a bit.

A guy meets the girl he had a crush on in high school, but she wouldn't give him the time of day then because he was the geeky, creepy son of a mortician and she was the head cheerleader and wouldn't be caught dead even talking to him. (Longer and still vague, but we're heading toward something.)

A guy who used to be nerdy in high school but is now handsome and rich meets the girl he loved in high school. Only now she's lost her looks, weighs 200 pounds, has bad hair, bad skin, and needs a kidney transplant and works the late shift at a factory where she lost a finger in a freak accident. When the guy buys the factory, he realizes that this woman is the girl he once loved. And the thing is, he *still* loves her. All his success meant nothing, so he decides to try again. But she still thinks he's a *geek* and still rejects him. He decides to try and win her over.

That is by no means a Vague Idea. And it's stronger than a Basic Premise. And there's enough plot in that long paragraph to give a sense of where the story will go.

The next step is to write the three-act storyline. But before getting to the storyline, it's important to point out that the hardest part of writing the storyline is pinpointing how the story will end.

You have to come up with an ending to something you haven't even begun writing yet, something you haven't even thought about other than a momentary surge of inspiration. It's like trying to figure out on Monday morning what you want for dessert at dinner on Friday night.

The only way to accomplish this is by pushing yourself to think things through. It's a bitch, but it can be done. And once you know how, you're closer to having a destination. And the destination is to know how your story is going to end.

Even in the storyline I just created, what's missing is how it will end. I don't know yet for sure. Will he win her over? Will he pursue and help her get her life back in order? Will she fall for him?

This is the hard part. I'm like the drunken frat boys who find themselves in the middle of nowhere without money, credit cards, gasoline, a map, or a plan.

And this is where the work begins.

As a simple exercise, *you* end my story. But give me three endings. One happy. One sad. One absurd.

Why three possible endings? Each will be different and will create its own unique tone that will affect your thinking when you actually begin writing the screenplay.

If in the sad ending you know the main character will die, you'll write the script one way. If you know the woman will die in his arms and that he'll be devastated, you'll write the script another way. If it's a big Hollywood ending, it'll be written in yet another way.

Above all, through this tiny collaboration of ours, we will have a beginning, a middle and an ending.

We will have a map for the 115-or-so-page journey that we would take if we were going to actually write the screenplay.

In the next chapter you'll see how I took the vague idea for *Little Helpers* and expanded it into an eight-page three-act storyline.

Nugget

Lost in Pennsylvania

From my apartment in New York City to my mother's home in northeastern Ohio, door to door, it's a 10-hour drive. That breaks down like this: two hours through New Jersey to the Pennsylvania border, six and a half hours through Pennsylvania to the Ohio border, and another 90 minutes to my mother's house.

This 10-hour drive pretty much reflects how a screenplay is structured. I came up with this little theory the first time I drove and I realized that when you take I-80 you are in the middle of Pennsylvania when you hit a town called Bellefonte. I remember the name only because of its similarity to the name of the singer Harry Belafonte.

I use this anecdote simply because I was working on a screenplay at the time and I hit a brick wall on page 55, roughly the middle of the second act. Most of my students hit a brick wall in the middle of Act Two. I came to describe this phenomenon as being lost in Pennsylvania. It *will* happen. There *will* be a wall. You *will* find a way to break through it.

■ ■ ■ ■ ■ ■

CHAPTER 11

If You Don't Know Where You Are Going, You Will End Up Somewhere Else

"Do not turn back when you are just at the goal."

PUBLILIUS SYRUS

The key word here is *destination*. The vaguest of ideas and the most expanded of premises mean nothing unless the storyline ends with a resolution. Pinpointing the resolution at this early stage is where most screenwriters have problems.

"How can I know how it will end before I even start writing?" is the most common refrain.

The answer is to force yourself to come up with a probable resolution to the story, if for no other reason than to give yourself a destination.

It's like those frat boys who take off on the cross-country trip without 10 seconds of preparation versus the frat boys who plan their junket. The guys with money, gas, clothing, places to stay, and a map are better suited for travel than the others.

Neither set of frat boys might get to where they're going as planned, just like you might wind up in a different—and better—place than your storyline indicated. But to write blindly without any sense of where you're going is just as foolhardy as jumping into your car at three in the morning and going somewhere.

The following takes you step by step through the process of defining the initial Vague Idea, expanding it into the Basic

Premise, then spreading it out into a three-act storyline with a beginning, middle, and ending.

"Little Helpers"
by D. B. Gilles

VAGUE IDEA
An elf is denied employment by Santa Claus because he's too tall.

BASIC PREMISE
An elf is denied employment by Santa Claus because he's too tall, so he leaves the North Pole, goes to New York, and hires a lawyer to sue Santa for job discrimination.

THREE-ACT STORYLINE

ACT ONE
At 6 feet 5 inches, Elvin, the son of two normal-sized elves, has grown way beyond the official height to become an elf. He is informed that because of his size he cannot be an elf. (**Instigating Event.**) The problem is that being an elf is all he ever wanted to be. He's devastated.

Not only that, he's the son, grandson, great-grandson, and great-great-grandson of elves, so to not be one breaks a family tradition.

Elvin is a sweetheart, a gentle giant. He accepts his fate. But his father, Elmore, a contentious little prick who hates being an elf and has always been a thorn in Santa's side, is a doting father who raised Elvin alone after his wife died.

Despite his own distaste at being an elf, in an effort to help Elvin and as an excuse to get away from the North Pole, which he despises (he'd rather live in Vegas, where the action is), Elmore decides that the only recourse Elvin has is to hire a lawyer to sue Santa Claus for job discrimination. (**Major Dramatic Question: Will they successfully sue Santa Claus and, if so, will Elvin get to be an elf?**)

Elvin and Elmore leave the North Pole and go to New York to find a lawyer. The problem is that no reputable attorney will take their case because no one believes them when they say they're elves. (**Complication.**)

Their appearance doesn't help. Elvin, at 6 feet 5, and Elmore, at 5 feet 3 (both dressed like elves are traditionally perceived), look more like members of a sideshow in a traveling carnival. (**Complication.**)

Finally they find a lawyer who will take their case and sue Santa Claus.

Elmore meets him at a strip bar. Not a good sign. (**Complication.**)

His name is Art Papparrazzi. He is the quintessential ambulance-chasing, shifty lawyer. Art is also Scrooge-like, angry and a *small man* who has always hated the concept of Christmas and Santa Claus. Art takes the case not so much because he wants to help Elvin, but because he figures there is a fortune to be made as the man who brings down Santa. ? (**Will he pull it off?**)

END OF ACT ONE

ACT TWO

But suing the big guy from the North Pole is easier said than done. Santa Claus hires a high-powered New York law firm with instructions to settle the case out of court. Under no circumstances does Santa want to be in a courtroom. (**Complication.**)

A crack legal team of three men and one woman is put together. The female lawyer is Rhonda Sweet, a drop-dead gorgeous redhead nearly six feet tall.

Rhonda's assignment has less to do with her talents as a lawyer than with her looks. After a quick background check on Art, Santa's defense team figures that because Art is so financially desperate, getting him to agree to an out-of-court settlement will be a snap.

They also know that he has a weak spot for the ladies, so Rhonda is assigned to be the liaison between Santa's defense team and Art.

From their initial meeting, Rhonda flirts with Art, and he is instantly attracted to her. She pretends to like him and they begin dating. (**Introduction of the Romantic Subplot.**)

Also falling for Rhonda is Elmore. But as a 5-feet-3-inch elf, he knows the 5-feet-10 Rhonda is out of his league.

Rhonda begins encouraging Art to settle the case out of court for a hefty sum. Through Rhonda's urgings, and because he thinks that by pleasing her he'll have a shot at her, Art agrees to a financial settlement that gives him a million dollars and Elvin two million—in lieu of Elvin having the chance to be an elf.

When Art tells this to Elmore and Elvin, Elmore is also tempted to settle. He sees the big money as an opportunity to change his life, get out of the North Pole, and head to Vegas.

But Elvin, no longer the gentle giant and now ticked off, refuses to agree. Art and Elmore try to convince him, but he won't budge. (**Complication.**)

Elvin wants to be an elf. It's not about money.

(And without getting schmaltzy, this is the theme of the story: People shouldn't be judged by how they look.)

When Art tells Rhonda that Elvin won't go for the deal, he elaborates on how Elvin's purity of desire in wanting to be an elf moves him. Rhonda is surprisingly unsympathetic, saying that just because somebody wants something doesn't mean he can get it. She reveals that she wanted to be something other than a lawyer and it didn't happen, so why should she feel sorry for Elvin?

When Art says that in the interest of serving his client, he has to turn down the out-of-court settlement, Rhonda loses her cool and lets it slip that she was only pretending to be interested in him.

This hurts and infuriates Art. He really thought she liked him. (**Complication.**)

Whatever spark of humanity is left within him prompts Art to apologize to Elvin and vow to go full force into actually going to trial.

In a scene with Elvin, Art tells the story of how he became a lawyer. In short, it began by watching *Perry Mason,* then *Ironside* and every TV lawyer show. But he was discouraged from being a lawyer by family and teachers because of his appearance.

Due to his diminutive size, he was told that he would never be able to win over a jury. "You're too short, too ugly, and you're bald."

Although Art went to law school and passed the bar exam, all the criticism and negativity took hold. He lost his confidence and instead of trying to become the great trial attorney he'd dreamed about, he turned bitter and desperate and wound up chasing ambulances and handling lowlifes. (**Art's Internal Conflict and Motivation.**)

He admits to Elvin that suing and interrogating Santa Claus will be the turning point of his mediocre career.

Will he pull it off and win the case for Elvin? !

END OF ACT TWO

ACT THREE

The lawsuit against Santa Claus is formally filed, and Santa himself is subpoenaed.

Meanwhile, with Art now the sworn enemy of Rhonda, *another* romantic subplot begins.

Elmore, who loves the action of New York, wanders into a small nightclub. Who does he see singing? None other than Rhonda.

She has a sultry, sexy singing style and a terrific voice. He approaches her but doesn't let on that he's Elvin's father or that he knows she's one of Santa's lawyers.

He finds out that Rhonda hates being an attorney and that what she's always wanted to be was a singer. She became a lawyer because it was expected of her by her family. He confides to her that he understands completely, adding that he's in a profession that he hates but is stuck with because it was expected of him.

He doesn't admit to being one of Santa's elves. Instead, he says he works as a consultant to Donald Trump.

As we build to the trial, we concentrate on the blossoming romance of Rhonda and Elmore and Art's intensive preparation for the trial. Instead of the sleazy lawyer we saw when we first met him, we now see a focused professional poring through law books, filing motions and briefs, and essentially working until he drops. Elvin, a computer whiz, pitches in and helps.

The trial begins. Santa and his lawyers on one side. Art and Elvin on the other.

Art is nervous and exhausted. He looks terrible. He doesn't even have a decent suit and looks like a bum compared to Santa's high-priced legal team. (**Complication.**)

Art does poorly, getting outclassed by the defense team. The confidence he had built up is now deflated. Santa's lawyers make another offer for a cash settlement. Art takes the offer back to Elvin. It's now $5 million.

Elvin says, "I don't want money. I want to be an elf. It's all I ever wanted to be." And then Elvin says, "Just like all you ever wanted to be is a great lawyer. This is your chance. If you're as good as you think you are . . . get me mine."

Bolstered by Elvin, Art turns down the cash settlement and goes back into court, determined to win the case.

We build to the big moment: Santa Claus takes the stand. (**Obligatory Scene/The Showdown.**) It's huge news. Court TV covers it. All the networks and the legal experts made famous during the Simpson trial are covering it. We cut from commentator to commentator.

Art knows he has to handle Santa Claus with kid gloves. He does a good job. But he knows that his real chance will be in his closing argument to the jury.

It finally comes. He speaks to the jury. The thrust of his rousing summation is how people should not be judged by the way they look.

"Why can't elves be tall?" (He points to Elvin.)

"Why can't lawyers be singers?" (He points to Rhonda.)

"Why can't an elf not be an elf?" (He points to Elmore.)

"Why can't a short, bald man be a great lawyer?" (He points to himself.)

Art then turns to Santa Claus and makes a personal plea to him on behalf of Elvin and manages to convince Santa to bend the rule and let Elvin be an elf.

Art finishes. He was brilliant.

The judge is about to charge the jury, but then . . .

Santa Claus stands up and says, "Maybe even an old guy like me can change his ways." He walks to Elvin, puts his arm around him, and says, "We'll try to find something for you."

The case is over. Art has won.

Elvin returns to the North Pole a full-fledged elf. Turns out he's a computer whiz, and he creates a new high-tech electronic division staffed entirely by oversized elves.

Art, because of his success at the trial, is now in a classy Central Park South office with a magnificent view of Manhattan. Well dressed and debonair, he is now one of the most sought-after lawyers in the country.

Final Scene:

Rhonda slinks out onto a stage in Las Vegas and sings.

In the audience is Elmore smoking a big cigar.

He's her manager and husband.

THE END

This is now beyond the Vague Idea and Basic Premise. After reading this storyline, you can see where the story will go once it's time to start writing the script.

For some screenwriters, this is enough. For others, there's still more to do. You probably won't know which category you'll fall into until you've tried to write a long treatment. In my experience, people either like doing them or hate the process.

If you're the kind of screenwriter who finds comfort in thinking things through and knowing exactly where your storyline is going before plowing into the screenplay, the next step is to write a full-scale treatment ranging in length from 15 to 35 pages.

If the three-act storyline for *Little Helpers* is detailed enough to give you an idea of where the screenplay will go, imagine how detailed a 15-, 20-, or 35-page treatment would be. Besides the narrative of the story, dialogue would be included, characters would be better defined, and subplots expanded, eliminated, or reduced.

I can't emphasize this enough: Long treatments aren't for everyone. But I feel adamantly that everyone should do a three-act storyline. To just "start writing" is folly.

And as one of my heroes, Dr. Laurence Peter, coauthor of *The Peter Principle,* said so eloquently, "If you don't know where you are going, you will end up somewhere else."

Nugget

The Heat That Melts Butter Hardens Steel

This Yiddish saying helps to make sense of why the same tragedy affects people differently.

There's a terrible car accident. Two friends. Both

survive but become paraplegics. One is filled
with rage, turns bitter, and hates being alive. The
other is grateful to be alive, learns to appreciate
all the things he can do, and rolls with the punch.
Either way, there's the beginning of the creation
of a character, and both would be interesting.
One woman who is raped is shamed by the
assault, keeps it to herself, and tries to live as if
nothing is wrong. Another rape victim becomes
empowered, is unashamed, confronts her
attacker, presses charges, bravely takes him to
court, and sees justice through. Stories are to be
found in the way people handle the cards they
are dealt.

A Few Thoughts on Outlines

"A preliminary account of a project. A plan. The line that bounds and gives form to something."

COMMON DICTIONARY DEFINITION

An outline can be an excellent blueprint for a screenplay, but I think it's better to do three-act storylines. The problem is that sometimes an outline is all you can manage to churn out. Pinpointing act breaks is difficult because at this early stage of the process it might be impossible to know where the structure will fall. Therefore, think of your outline as a three-act storyline but without the act breaks. An outline is usually a few pages, from one to maybe five. There are those who might call something two or three pages long a treatment, but to me a treatment must be longer and have act breaks and a much more realized vision of the story.

However, once you've put an outline on paper, it's crucial to move on to a three-act storyline.

The following outline is four pages long in manuscript. You get a fairly solid glimpse of what the big picture will be. I wasn't sure where the act breaks came, but I felt confident that what's here was enough to give someone an idea of what the story could be.

OUTLINE
"SPENT"
by D. B. Gilles

VAGUE IDEA

Out-of-control spendaholic is romanced and then blackmailed by a collection-agency shark.

OUTLINE

A 32-year-old executive who is an out-of-control spendaholic is up for a big promotion. (**Instigating Event and Major Dramatic Question: Will she get the promotion?**) Only problem is that a background check must show that she's financially sound and has impeccable character. (**Complication.**)

Her name is Gretchen Hobbs, and her credit rating is a disaster. She's maxed out on numerous credit cards, behind on loans, and on the verge of foreclosure on her house. If the truth were discovered, she'd never stand a chance.

Because the new job means a huge salary increase—which is her primary reason for wanting it—she's driven to do whatever it takes to clean up her credit rating and overall financial impression. It's important to know that although she's a spendaholic, she's extremely talented and a hard worker.

She goes to a consultant, who tells her among other things to join Debtors Anonymous and to contact all of her creditors and get it on paper that she's attempting to resolve her debts.

She joins Debtors Anonymous, but only halfheartedly. She views it as a necessary evil, and she doesn't even go to all the meetings.

She also doesn't see herself as being as bad as the other members and, of course, she is totally in denial. We'll learn that her irresponsibility with money ruined her first marriage and destroyed two other relationships.

As she goes about reconciling her debts and preparing for the job interview, we see how truly irresponsible she is when it comes to money.

Call it a case of *bigshotitis*, buying expensive clothes then losing interest in them, having a pricey car, collecting antiques, buying gifts, picking up tabs at expensive restaurants—you name it.

Things go fine until she contacts a guy at a collection agency handling one of her outstanding debts in the amount of $19,000. (**Pivotal Plot Point.**)

When she asks him about working something out, he rejects the idea outright because she's been dodging his phone calls and correspondence for months.

Further shocking her, he knows about every one of her debts because he's gotten her credit report and knows her entire credit and financial history.

He calls her a deadbeat. She hangs up on him.

But then he calls her back, says he's looked over her file, and suggests that she come by for a meeting to discuss her situation. He gives her an address. But the address turns out to be a restaurant, and the "meeting" turns out to be lunch. (**Pivotal Plot Point.**)

But he's nice-looking and rather charming. It would be easy for her to be attracted to him.

During lunch the guy offers her a curious deal: Go out on a date with him, and he'll think about cutting her some slack on her debt. (**Pivotal Plot Point.**)

At first, she rejects the idea categorically and storms out of the restaurant. But as she gets closer and closer to the job interview, and as she makes arrangements with her other debtors, it's clear that this one guy is going to be the only obstacle.

She agrees to the date. It's pleasant, fun. But she has an agenda, so at the end of the evening, she asks him what the arrangement will be regarding her $19,000 bill.

He says he needs more time to think about it, adding that he will also require not only another date, but a kiss good-night. The next date leads him to a second kiss and another date.

The upshot will finally be that he makes her a more concrete offer:

Sleep with him and he'll wipe away the entire debt. (**Pivotal Plot Point.**)

At first she's outraged. "I'm not a whore!" she screams. But after much deliberation and out of a desperate need to clear her credit rating and get the new job, she agrees.

They sleep together. (**Pivotal Plot Point.**) It's very romantic à la *Indecent Proposal*. She's even able to justify in her head that she likes the guy and he's not bad-looking.

The only problem is that he doesn't meet his end of the bargain. (**Pivotal Plot Point.**)

She's been had and she's devastated and there's nothing she can do now but realize how low she's gotten because of her financial dysfunction.

Meanwhile, the job interview comes. They do a credit check. She's found out and she doesn't get the promotion. (**Pivotal Plot Point.**)

Now, at long last humbled and with a sense of purpose, she goes to Debtors Anonymous. In her final action she'll get her revenge on the collection-agency guy by taking him to court. (**Pivotal Plot Point.**)

The film ends with her speaking before the Debtors Anonymous group and beginning her long journey back.

THE END

Short and sweet. Is there a movie somewhere in these pages? I'd say so. Is it a feature film? Frankly, I always saw it as a movie for television. But if the script got into an edgier territory with the protagonist having, say, a gambling or drug problem or a major sexual dysfunction, sure. I just saw it as a nifty little character study that takes a look at how a young successful woman can screw up her life because of her wild spending and how bad judgment can only add more havoc to an already prickly situation.

Use this as a model for a starting point to writing three-act storylines. It has a beginning, middle, and an ending. I didn't get into much nuance, shadings, and contours in plot or character, but this serves its purpose as an outline for deeper thinking and more meticulous plotting.

Nugget

People Are the Same Everywhere

I'm not especially well traveled, but I've been to a few places, and after living in New York City for more than 25 years, I've been exposed to enough people from different cities, countries, and cultures to believe that people are the same when it comes to the emotions and feelings that go with the territory of being human beings. That's why Americans enjoy foreign films. It's nice to know that the guy in France or Japan feels just like us when his heart's been broken. Or that the woman in Munich is in just as much turmoil as the woman in Ireland, Italy, or Mexico whose husband is unjustly accused of a crime. Throughout the world, American movies are, for all intents and purposes, foreign films. Whether the European market likes American movies or American movie stars is a separate issue, but even with subtitles, foreigners are identifying with stories by American screenwriters. Language, mores, and culture might be regional, but human emotions are universal. You're not writing for your neighborhood; you're writing for the world.

CHAPTER 13

Eccentrics,

or:

How That 7-Eleven Clerk With the Bad Eye Can Make Your Script Better

"Now here, you see, it takes all the running you can do to keep in the same place."

LEWIS CARROLL

Through the Looking Glass

The best stories are often about outcasts, eccentrics, misfits, loners, and people who aren't in the mainstream of life.

You know who they are. The woman who never marries and becomes a companion to her mother because her father is either dead, inattentive, or a drunk. Or maybe she's afraid to leave Mom because she's been warned ad nauseam that men are bastards, so to protect herself from being hurt like her mother was, she remains close to the hearth.

Then there's the son who got married and divorced and comes back and sticks around. And like his female counterpart, there's the son who never leaves or dates. He gains weight, takes care of his folks, or looks after his retarded brother, or tries to make a go of the struggling family business.

The two sisters (or brothers) who steer clear of marriage, manage to leave home, but avoid independence by becoming roommates. They rent until they're in their thirties, then as middle age looms and dating has ceased to happen and security becomes a new factor, they buy a place together and live platonically as a couple.

Have you ever wondered about the late-night clerk at the 7-Eleven with the weird overbite and bad eye? He dates the chubby girl with the mole on the tip of her nose who works the graveyard shift at the doughnut factory.

The 40-year-old woman in the church choir who sings like an angel but is so pathologically shy she can't talk to men, except priests, whom she views as holy and paternal because her own father was so emotionally distant and, of course, being priests, they're safe.

The lifer at the company, married to his job, whose personal life is so empty that he goes in on weekends but doesn't put in for overtime.

You know who I'm talking about. They're everywhere. Every family has at least one. Weird Uncle George who does odd jobs at a funeral home, coaches Little League, lives in an efficiency apartment over a friend's garage, and goes to science-fiction conventions. Creepy Aunt Bonnie who quotes Scripture and secretly downs a fifth of Jack Daniel's every night and calls in to local radio talk shows.

Cousin Bert who doesn't know he's gay.

And, of course, the people who are literally and physically out of the mainstream of life, the homeless. Not those who are mentally ill. The homeless man who interests me as a writer and student of human behavior is the one who is intelligent, cunning. The one who had the big job. Who made the big bucks. Who had the house in the suburbs and the whole nine yards. Why is this guy on the street?

In fact, a great film has already been made on this subject, *The Fisher King* with Robin Williams.

If you can't find an idea to get excited about or a character that interests you, look at the outcasts, eccentrics, and lost souls around you, not judgmentally but with curiosity and compassion. They're human beings too, but they live their lives way off the beaten path. If you have the courage to go down that path, you might find an incredible story to tell.

Nugget

Just Because It Really Happened Doesn't Mean It Belongs in Your Screenplay

Some people have no problem coming up with ideas to write about. Others have a difficult time finding any, so they make the mistake of writing about things that really happened to them. It's one thing to write a movie based on the camping trip your family took when you were 15 and your parents bonded with you and your brother and everyone returned home closer than ever. But if you write a script chronicling every moment the way it actually happened, you aren't writing a screenplay, you're making a documentary. A screenplay, like a novel and a play, is fiction. Made up. Maybe inspired by some real-life event, but largely made up. Go ahead and let that long-ago camping trip be the catalyst of a story, but add some dramatic spice by having an escaped convict show up and kidnap your mother. That way you, your brother, and your father can bond while trying to save Mom. I'm a firm believer that writers should write what they know. But being a writer means using your imagination to enhance and expand what you know. If you want to chronicle real events the way they happened, don't write screenplays. Make documentaries.

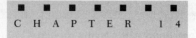

CHAPTER 14

The Weenie Surprise
and
the "Now What?" Factor

*"Knowledge must come through action; you can have no
test which is not fanciful, save by trial."*

SOPHOCLES

Making it through Acts One and Two are major victories, but most
screenplays run into trouble in the third act. This happens because
in constructing the story a screenwriter fails to keep building the
dramatic tension in Act Two to carry the reader to the next big high
point of the story.

As discussed earlier, think of Act Two as 50 to 60 pages of
complications, twists, turns, and wrinkles, all building to an event
that gives the reader an ! or new information.

Ideally this new information should come as a surprise to the
reader, something totally unexpected. Info that causes the reader
to smile, guffaw, or twitch from the shock of being fooled.

The best example of a second-act ending that I've ever seen is
from the Neil Jordan 1992 film *The Crying Game*.

The new information he provided his audience with has to do
with what I call the Weenie Surprise.

HERE'S THE STORYLINE:

An IRA splinter group has kidnapped a British soldier. A reluctant member of the group assigned to watch the prisoner befriends him. The prisoner carries on about his girlfriend in London, how badly he wants to be with her. But the prisoner is killed and the reluctant terrorist feels compelled to visit the girl in London and tell her of her boyfriend's death.

Only problem is, the terrorist falls in love with the girl, who is a singer in a nightclub.

As we build to the end of Act Two, the terrorist finds out that the girl is really a *guy*. We discover this when the two of them are about to make love for the first time.

We see the girl/guy's penis. Yikes! That's what I call new information.

The beauty of this powerful moment is that it gives the main character a moral dilemma to deal with for the rest of the story: Despite the fact that he is straight, he has come to love the girl/guy.

So what does he do?

If you haven't seen the film, I've spoiled the surprise at the end of Act Two, but I won't spoil the third act for you because the screenwriter fills it with enough additional twists and turns to culminate in a brilliantly satisfying ending.

Needless to say, this is an extreme example of a powerful end of Act Two event, but I believe the best examples are extreme because we never forget them.

Previously I dealt with the mathematics of structure. The end of Act One should come on or about page 30, the end of Act Two should come around page 82 to 90 (depending upon the length of your script), and Act Three should wrap up in 25 to 30 pages.

Never forget that as you're heading toward the end of Act Two, you *must* give us a big event/twist/surprise/reversal/piece of new information that will get its hooks in us and make us turn the pages to find out what's going to happen.

But what do you do if your story isn't sensational or outrageous and you can't rely on the appearance of an unexpected male organ?

No problem.

You have to use what I call

THE "NOW WHAT?" FACTOR

One great example from the late sixties:

The Graduate (1967)

A 21-year-old college grad (Dustin Hoffman) starts a purely sexual affair with a 40-something woman (Anne Bancroft). She's a friend of his parents. She also has a college-age daughter (Katharine Ross). At the urging of his parents, Dustin Hoffman's character asks the daughter out on a date. He feels awkward, to say the least, but there's a spark.

Although the daughter is about to be married, he starts to see her while he continues to sleep with the mother. He reveals to the daughter that he's been having an affair with an older woman but tells the daughter that he's going to end it. He wants to see the daughter.

The tension is building because the mother has discovered that her daughter is interested in Hoffman. She confronts Hoffman and demands that he stay away from her daughter. They have a huge argument about this. Hoffman says no. The mother warns him that if he doesn't back off, *she* will tell her daughter.

Meanwhile, the daughter suddenly shows up. Hoffman knows that the jig is up. He hopes that if *he* tells the daughter first, she might be more forgiving.

So the big moment happens when the daughter and Hoffman are in his car. He's trying to tell her. And at the precise moment he is about to reveal the truth, the mother shows up.

Without a word being said, the daughter knows that the older woman Hoffman's been sleeping with is her own mother.

End of Act Two.

So where's the new information? What about the Weenie Surprise?

Actually most scripts don't build to something as outrageous as a drag queen to tweak its audience. So the next best thing is to give us a powerful moment or event that will grab us emotionally and make us say, "Now what?"

The "Now what?" at the end of Act Two of *The Graduate* gives us the emotional tug we need to watch the rest of the movie, which by this point has all sorts of problems.

Hoffman wants the daughter. But she hates him for sleeping with her mother, and she's going ahead with her marriage (and we know that she and Hoffman are much more right for each other), and she and her mother aren't speaking, and Hoffman and the mother aren't sleeping together anymore, and the friendship between the two families is crumbling, and Hoffman and the mother are now dealing with the guilt and immorality of what they did, and on top of this we like Hoffman and the daughter and we *really* want them to get together.

So how does it end? Go rent the movie.

Never forget that an audience is willing to go along with you to the very end as long as you keep giving them surprises. Some screenplays hook us from the opening moments and never let go. Others take their time and seduce us slowly before winning over our hearts and minds. But the best screenplays grab us, take us for a whirlwind roller-coaster ride, and never let go.

Nugget

Stories Are About
People in Situations

The situations can be funny, embarrassing, sad, dangerous, tragic, epic, mundane, menacing— you name it. And the person in the situation must not want to be there. But he *has* to be there. He has no choice. This is often called *the reluctant hero*. Maybe he's brought to a situation by circumstances out of his control or by his reckless behavior. On the other hand, if he wants to be in the situation initially, he must soon want to get out. But he can't. He's stuck.

CHAPTER 15

The Case of the Missing Third Act,

or:

Is It Over *Already?*

"Always be closing."

SALESMAN'S SAYING

Sometimes a script can build to a terrific end of Act Two only to crash and burn in Act Three.

The problem is that the Major Dramatic Question of the story is resolved too quickly.

Late for Dinner (1991)

Two guys in 1962 get themselves cryogenically frozen for what should be one night, but due to some major complications, it turns into 29 years.

The main character is 25 and has an infant daughter. So when he and his pal wake up he's *still* 25, but his beloved wife is pushing 55, and his young daughter is almost the same age as he was when he "left."

We learn that both mother and daughter always assumed he took off and abandoned them back in 1962. They went on with their lives.

The plot boils down to the guy finding a way to convince his wife and daughter that he has indeed returned after being frozen for 29 years.

As goofy as this sounds, the execution worked. After suspending your disbelief, you go with it and you root for the guy to somehow convince these adult women that it's really him.

There are plenty of complications and twists along the way, but the story builds nicely to the big moment when the 25-year-old hero finally convinces the 55-year-old woman (who looks more like his mother than the young woman he married 29 years before) that he is indeed who he says he is.

They kiss.

It's very moving and touching.

I said to myself, "A perfect way to end Act Two."

But guess what? As they're kissing, the credits start to roll. The movie is over.

I felt cheated.

To me, the real story was just beginning, namely: How will this couple, once very much in love when they were both young, get along after all this time? She has 29 years of life on him. He's still 25, and he hasn't the slightest idea of all the changes in society since he was frozen, let alone the changes that certainly occurred in his wife.

To me, the third act should have dealt with the problems this couple would realistically have faced. That would have been dramatic and satisfying.

Instead, I left the theater unsatisfied and ticked off at the screenwriters. But sometimes you see a movie that ends abruptly and doesn't tie up loose ends yet leaves you wanting nothing and strangely satisfied.

This approach to screenwriting might be described like this:

IT HAS A NICE BEAT
AND YOU CAN DANCE TO IT

The Full Monty (1997)

Two unemployed, down-on-their-luck British working-class guys observe how the local women spend money to watch some Chippendales-like dancers strip down to their drawers. They get the idea to do the same with the exception that they will drop their drawers completely (referred to in Britain as showing "the full Monty"). These two set out to find a few others to join them and, despite personal problems in their own lives, eventually rent a pub, dance, and drop their drawers.

The End. Fini. That's all, folks.

Any way you look at it, it's over.

The writer had his characters do what he said they would do.

We didn't follow up on what happened to the protagonists or whether they were going to be all right or whether the one guy would get back with his wife or whether the other would get custody of his child or anything.

It just *ended,* and millions of people the world over walked out of the theater satisfied.

And believe me, if you haven't seen the movie, it ended quite unexpectedly, with a freeze-frame rear shot of the five naked guys. It ended just as abruptly as *Late for Dinner,* but *The Full Monty* worked.

The plot was simple and clear. The heroes were very human. Regular guys. None of them pretty boys. One was fat. Each was in a bad place in his life, and they weren't that young. Regular folks the world over identified with these guys.

It wasn't *Citizen Kane* or *Schindler's List* or *Doctor Zhivago* or *Raging Bull* or anywhere near a great film or a great script. It was, well, it was sweet. And nice. And fun.

And like the kids used to say on *American Bandstand,* "It had a nice beat and you can dance to it."

Late for Dinner was too hard to dance to.

Another problem was that *Late for Dinner* didn't set the tone it was going to follow early on.

Setting the tone is another way of setting the rules of a game.

Late for Dinner presented itself as a high-concept love story. It failed because it thought the concept would carry the day, when in reality in love stories it's the *romance* that people remember.

(*Think fast*: What was the plot of *Casablanca*? Unless it tripped off your tongue, you won't remember. But I bet you remember the love story. Bogart is running a bar, and his life is turned upside down when Ingrid Bergman, the lost love of his life, walks in. "Of all the gin joints in the world she has to come into mine." From that moment on all we care about is whether or not they'll get back together.)

MAJOR DRAMATIC QUESTION OF "LATE FOR DINNER"
WILL THE GUY BE ABLE TO RECLAIM HIS WOMAN AFTER BEING FROZEN FOR 29 YEARS?
ANSWER
YES.

He came back and reclaimed her. But then he had to live with her and deal with her as a grown woman, with all her complexities and experiences and baggage.

Because Act Three never dealt with this, the audience was lost and the movie tanked.

WHY A WEAK THIRD ACT
IS LIKE BAD SEX

Writing a screenplay is not only telling a story, it's selling a story.

There's an old salesman's maxim: Always be closing.

Roughly translated, it means a good salesman must relentlessly push his client to buy.

As a screenwriter, you must relentlessly push your audience to "buy" what you're giving them on the pages of your script.

You start the sale by luring your audience in and hopefully hook them immediately with the expectation of a nifty tale to come (Act One). Then you let them settle in and take a slow but ever-intensifying uphill ride in a roller coaster that rests for a brief moment on the top of the tracks where there's no turning back and nowhere to go but full steam ahead into the final stages of the world into which you've ensnared them (Act Two).

Now comes the closing part.

Think of Act Three as the symbolic ride down the roller coaster. Like the real thing, the ride down has to be faster and more exhilarating than the ride up. The ride up is all about expectation, possibilities, and anticipation.

The ride down is about getting questions answered, new questions posed, finding relief from the tension you've felt and ultimately satisfaction.

A strong "close" by a good salesman results in the sale. He's happy. The client's happy. They're each getting something out of the time they've spent together.

A weak close means the salesman's lost the sale. Maybe he lost his concentration or took the client for granted or lost his confidence or showed his desperation or just ran out of steam.

Whatever, the sale is gone.

But a strong third act is like the good close. You and your audience are happy, and you've both gotten something out of the time you spent together. Which is why a weak third act is like bad sex: It happens too fast, takes too long, or doesn't even get you turned on.

[Personal note to the makers of *Late for Dinner*: I loved it until the kiss.]

Nugget

Act Two and a Half

Think of this as the second exclamation point—
an event occurring in approximately the last
five minutes of a script that sends the story
into yet another new and surprising, unexpected direction. A variation on this with
regard to character arc comes from the
renowned Russian acting teacher Konstantin
Stanislavski, who said that the last 90 seconds
of a play are the most important for the protagonist because it is during this time that the
main character experiences an irreversible
moment of truth. He realizes there's no turning back. The die is cast. And simultaneously
he goes into a new sense of awareness. To
observe great examples of this, rent the following films and examine the last five minutes: *Schindler's List*, *One Flew Over the
Cuckoo's Nest*, *It's a Wonderful Life*, *On the
Waterfront*, *Seven Beauties*, and *Rain Man*.

CHAPTER 16

The Importance of Treatments

"An original story written for motion picture purposes in a form suitable for use as the basis of a screenplay."

DEFINITION OF A TREATMENT

You might not want to do a treatment, but the day will come when you will have to. You've written a screenplay that gets you an agent or some attention from a producer. They like your script, but they don't want to make it. But they want to work with you.

Treatments either give you a Vague Idea for something. Or you give them one. Maybe you have a premise or an outline or even a three-act storyline.

Bottom line, they like what you have and want to go forward. Odds are, they'll want you to do a treatment before you start the script. Many writers have "pitch" meetings in which they talk out concepts and ideas. Some writers get deals on the pitch alone. But before they start the screenplay, many will have to turn in a treatment first.

That's why it's important to learn how to do one.

The nature of a treatment is such that it lays out the entire storyline in essentially narrative form. There is some dialogue, but not that much, just snippets here and there to get across the point of a scene. If I were to set out to write the screenplay, I would have a tightly detailed blueprint to follow.

This is not to say that I wouldn't veer from what's here. But I might. A scene might not work. An idea for a scene or plot twist that I hadn't thought of might pop into my head and take me in another direction.

Most important, the treatment is ready to be turned into a screenplay. Key characters are here, the motivation of the major characters is established, the act breaks come at the right places, and I know how it's going to end.

Use this as a guide for any length treatment you will write.

TREATMENT
"Long After Dark"
by D. B. Gilles

BASIC PREMISE

A troubled 17-year-old female high-school student helps her new neighbor, a 36-year-old woman living with her abusive mother, discover a shocking secret about her true identity—that she might be a kidnap victim.

ACT ONE

Introduce Sina Hobbs, 36, never married, never left home, and never had a relationship (or even a date), lives with her 60-year-old mother. She's overweight, looks older than her 36 years, and has a perpetual beaten-down look.

Introduce 17-year-old Amy Kent and her father, Lew, as they move into the house next door. (**Instigating Event: If they didn't move into this particular house in this particular neighborhood, the story wouldn't have happened.**) It's a small working-class Midwestern town—kind of in between country and suburb. Lew has relocated here for a job. He and Amy don't know a soul. Amy's mother, with whom she was very close, died two years ago.

Amy's depression over her mother's passing, combined with a lifelong shyness, has turned her into a reclusive bookworm. Too shy to attempt to make friends, she sticks close to home, taking care of the house, the yard, cooking supper for her father, etc. (**Preparation for Amy to view Sina as a mother-substitute/mother-figure.**)

Amy first sees Sina on moving day, shyly peeking through a window. Sina waves, but as Amy is about to wave back, Sina's mother, Marion Hobbs, tough and unfriendly, appears in the window and abruptly pulls her away. (**Complication/ obstacle in the way of a friendship between Sina and Amy.**) The sight of a grown woman being treated so rudely jolts Amy. *What's going on next door?*

Amy's father starts his job. Amy settles into her new life, which means she's alone until Dad gets home from work. Other than daily visits to the library, Amy finds herself at loose ends. She becomes drawn to Sina, whom she observes in her yard, tending a garden, feeding birds, etc. And Sina's sweet, gentle ways remind Amy of her own mother. (**More preparation for Amy to get close to Sina and want to help her later.**)

Amy also hears snippets of conversation between Sina and her mother. Mainly it's constant criticism of Sina. Amy feels sympathy for Sina. (**Further motivation for Amy to get to know Sina.**)

We go into Sina's house and observe the odd relationship between this mother and daughter. Sina is treated as if she were hired help. And she never seems to do anything right. We see that Marion Hobbs is a heavy smoker who likes her beer and has a bit of a gambling problem. She looks like she could be a waitress in a rough roadside trucker bar.

Amy isn't sure if Sina is retarded or slow or what. (**Amy's primary dramatic action: to find out what, if anything, is wrong with Sina.**) She tries to make contact with Sina in their adjoining backyards. Just as they introduce themselves, Sina's mother angrily calls Sina into the house. Sina, frightened, runs away from Amy. Fascinated by this peculiar mother–daughter relationship, Amy is further motivated to find out what makes it tick.

Amy observes that Sina's mother leaves the house at midafternoon to go to work. We'll learn that she works the afternoon shift at a factory. Amy waits until Mrs. Hobbs leaves one day, then knocks on Sina's door.

From inside the house, Sina sees Amy, but she's afraid to answer the door. She even touches the doorknob, but at the last second, she backs away. Amy goes home. (**An obstacle that Amy must circumvent.**)

Amy next tries to formally meet Sina by calling on her *and* her mother. Mrs. Hobbs answers the door, is unfriendly, and doesn't encourage the possibility of a friendship. Sina overhears the conversation. She goes to her mother and asks why she can't have a friend. Mrs. Hobbs dismisses the issue.

Later, as Amy works in the backyard, clearing away the bushes and weeds that separate the two homes, she cuts her hand with a garden tool. Suddenly Sina appears and helps Amy take care of the wound. Contact is made, and the friendship takes its first baby steps. (**A believable, organic way for the two to meet that prepares the way for Amy to get to know Sina and learn more about her situation.**)

Amy learns more about Sina. She's by no means retarded. She's really a child-woman living under her dominating mother's scornful shadow. Sina admits that the only time she's happy is when her mother goes to work. While alone, Sina watches talk shows and reads showbiz magazines that she takes from neighbors' garbage.

Amy becomes very protective of Sina, and she's determined to help Sina be less controlled by her mother. (**Further motivation for Amy to get even more involved in Sina's life.**)

Sina's mother stares suspiciously out the window at Amy. She doesn't look pleased.

As Amy gets to know Sina, she learns that Sina has lived in the same house her entire life, has no memories of a father, and dropped out of school at 16. Sina seldom leaves the house alone, usually only to walk to a nearby grocery store for supplies.

Amy's love of reading and learning propels her to share it with Sina. She realizes that Sina reads on the level of a fifth grader. She blames Sina's mother for this. She offers to help Sina improve her reading skills. (**Further motivation for Amy to get more involved in Sina's life.**)

The more Amy learns of Sina's mother's control, the more she feels compelled to help Sina get out from under her mother's dominance. (**Amy's primary dramatic action has now changed. She now is determined to help set Sina free. Also, Major Dramatic Question introduced.**) Besides helping Sina improve her reading skills, Amy suggests more visible forms of rebellion like how Sina dresses (old and frumpy) and her eating habits (mainly junk food), losing weight, etc.

Sina's mother notices subtle changes in Sina, and she knows who's to blame. Mrs. Hobbs shows up at Amy's house, only Amy's not home. But her father is. She demands that Lew tell Amy to back off from Sina. (**Another obstacle for Amy.**) She tells a story of how Sina had an accident as a child, injuring her head, and that she was never the same. The mother gives a convincing sob story, saying that Sina is simple-minded and that over the years a number of people have tried to help her, but it hasn't worked.

As the mother is speaking, Amy comes home and hears much of what she's saying. Politely, Amy tries to reason with Mrs. Hobbs, but Lew discourages this. Sina's mother leaves. Lew tells Amy to stay away from Sina. (**Another obstacle for Amy.**) They argue. He warns her about the danger of sticking your nose into other people's problems, even if you're convinced it's for the best. Amy, filled with the idealism of youth, resists what her father is saying. (**Potential conflict between Amy and her father.**)

The next day, Sina comes over. Amy tells Sina about her mother's visit, pointing out what her mother said about Sina's childhood accident. Sina says that she never injured her head as a child. (**Key information. Amy now knows Sina's mother is lying.**) Amy tells Sina that they'd better cool their meetings for a while. This makes Sina angry. She storms out, goes home, and, for the first time in her life, challenges her mother.

Amy hears the screaming. It's ugly. Then it stops. Amy is pleased that Sina has finally spoken up. But then Amy hears Sina screaming hysterically. Amy runs to Sina's house. Sina's mother has collapsed. (**Heightened moment to end the act.**)

?

ACT TWO

Sina's mother is in a coma. She has had a stroke. This is bad for Sina because she has no other relatives and no friends. (**Major complication for Sina and indirectly for Amy.**) Alone for the first time in her life, Sina must learn to get along without her mother, not only in the outside world, but in her own world.

Even though Sina is used to cooking and cleaning, she isn't used to being completely alone. Nothing makes sense to her. Desperate, she turns to Amy for help. (**Logical, natural way to further involve Amy.**)

Amy can't say no, despite her father's warning to remain uninvolved. She identifies with Sina because she too is having a difficult time adapting to life without *her* mother.

At first, Sina is like a helpless child, unable to deal with the loneliness, especially her first night alone in the house. We learn that Sina has had a lifelong fear of the dark, especially the hours past midnight. She's petrified.

In the middle of the night, she knocks on Amy's door and begs to stay. Amy says okay. She cradles Sina in her arms. Lew, upset, says he'll allow it only this one night.

So begins Sina making a total pest of herself, bothering Amy constantly. (**Complication for subplot involving Amy's romance with Nelson.**)

And it couldn't have come at a worse time because Amy meets a boy, Nelson, also 17, and begins dating him. (We'll see them meeting at the library, where he works part time.)

Sina is jealous and possessive of Amy, much like a child who's angry that a parent is dating someone. She hates Nelson. Amy and Sina have an argument and Amy yells at Sina, who runs away in tears.

Amy goes to her father for advice. She's fearful of what will happen to Sina if her mother dies. Amy's dad brings up the reality that if Sina is unable to take care of herself, she might have to go into some kind of institution. He also suggests that despite her feelings for Sina, she's only asking for trouble by getting too involved. (**Creates minor conflict between Amy and her dad. She knows how he feels, yet she's compelled to follow her heart.**)

Amy tells Nelson about her concerns for Sina's future. He says that having Sina out of her life is the best thing that could've happened. He makes cruel remarks about Sina, filling her in on rumors about Sina. This angers Amy. She realizes Nelson's a jerk. She dumps him and goes to Sina's house to try to make up. (**Complication for Amy. She really thought Nelson was a good guy. A part of her wonders if he might be right.**)

The house is a mess. Sina has thrown a tantrum. Amy realizes that her father was right about not getting involved. (**An Internal Conflict arises for Amy. Should she stay or should she go?**) But she knows it's too late now, and she can't just walk out of Sina's life. And there's that nagging maternal longing.

Sina and Amy make up, and Amy has even more resolve to get Sina on the right track to a life. (**Now Amy is fully enmeshed in Sina's life.**) She encourages Sina to do three things: get her high-school equivalency degree, learn a skill so she can support herself in case her mother doesn't recover, and make an effort to find out if she has any relatives. Sina agrees and Amy promises to help her.

Amy also volunteers to help Sina dress and look more her age. And Amy convinces Sina that by being a stronger person, she'll be in a better frame of mind to care for her mother when she comes home.

Because the house is in such disarray, Amy helps Sina get started putting the place in order. Amy has to leave. Sina continues cleaning. While putting something away in the attic, Sina stumbles onto something locked away in an old suitcase stuck in her mother's bedroom. Inside are faded newspaper clippings from 35 years ago reporting the disappearance of a baby.

Sina realizes the horrible truth—*she was a kidnap victim*. (**Major Pivotal Plot Point revelation.**)

According to the newspaper clippings, which came from a small-town paper 300 miles away in another state, Sina's real name is Marjorie Tuttle. Her parents are Will and Linda Tuttle. Sina was kidnapped 35 years ago. But instead of calling Amy or the police, Sina tells no one. She falls asleep clutching the newspaper clippings.

!

ACT THREE

Obsessed with the information in the newspaper clippings, Sina decides she wants to see Mrs. Hobbs. Although she has never gone far from home alone, Sina sets out to visit her mother. She doesn't drive, so she must walk part of the way, then take a bus.

She gets to the hospital, the newspaper clippings with her. She tries to communicate with her still-comatose mother, asking her what the clippings mean, who she really is, and the biggest question of all: *Did you kidnap me?*

Sina asks a few more questions, and we realize that she is torn. She knows that kidnapping is a serious crime, but as Marion Hobbs is the only family she has ever known, Sina has mixed feelings about what to do. (**Plays up Sina's Internal Conflict.**)

Sina stays until visiting hours are over. Before she leaves, she whispers to her mother, "I wish you could wake up so you could tell me that you didn't kidnap me. If you did, they'll take you to jail."

It's late and getting home presents a problem. Sina takes the wrong bus and winds up at the end of the line. Lost, confused, and frightened, she causes a scene in a store. The police are called and take her to jail.

Amy gets a call from the police. She and her father pick Sina up. Sina is afraid to stay alone in the house. She stays at Amy's that night. Amy notices that Sina is behaving differently. She seems preoccupied. Amy asks what's bothering Sina. Sina says nothing.

Sina is watching a children's program. It's about police, specifically how people should trust the police.

Later, Sina walks to the grocery store. While there she sees a cop. Recalling what she just heard about trusting police, she brings up the newspaper clippings and her concern that she might be a kidnap victim.

Like most people in the town, the cop knows Sina and assumes that she is mildly retarded. That, combined with the way she speaks and her nervousness, makes him slough off what she says about being kidnapped, thinking that they're just ramblings. He even does something of a head trip on her, pointing out, "You should be ashamed for even thinking these thoughts." (**Major complication.**)

Indeed ashamed and more confused than ever, Sina loses herself in one of her talk shows. One in particular is about finding missing persons. There's an 800 number from a detective on the show. (**Key Pivotal Plot Point.**) Sina calls the number. Reaches the guy. Because she has such a childlike way of speaking and because she's nervous, the detective thinks it's a crank call from a little kid. He hangs up on her. (**Complication.**)

Sina finally decides to tell Amy. In fact, she's walking out the door, headed for Amy's house, when the phone rings. It's the hospital. Mrs. Hobbs has regained consciousness. Sina holds off telling Amy about the newspaper clippings.

Mrs. Hobbs comes home. Sina is ready to confront her with the newspaper clippings. But because of their codependency, Sina is ecstatic to see her. And because she's weak, Mrs. Hobbs is unusually sweet to Sina. Happy with this new treatment, Sina puts away the clippings. (**Key event that prolongs the dramatic tension.**)

Although Mrs. Hobbs has been in the hospital for only a short time, she notices a change in Sina: new look, new clothes, new attitude.

Mrs. Hobbs doesn't know how to take it, but now she really needs Sina. She's kinder and less critical. (**Key dramatic action that makes us wonder if things will work themselves out between mother and daughter.**)

Amy remarks how happy Sina seems. Sina explains that since her mother got sick she's a lot nicer. Things go smoothly for a few days, then Mrs. Hobbs finds the newspaper clippings. (**Major Pivotal Plot Point.**) She storms into Sina's bedroom, demanding to know if Sina told anyone.

Sina says no. Meekly, she asks what happened 35 years ago. Mrs. Hobbs says, "Nothing. You're imagining everything. It wasn't you." Mrs. Hobbs is brutal. She intimidates Sina, saying that anyone who heard about this would misinterpret it. "I would go to jail, and you'd spend the rest of your life in the loony bin."

Sina promises not to say anything. Mrs. Hobbs then burns all the clippings. (**Complication: Now there is no evidence.**) Mrs. Hobbs demands to know if Sina's hiding anything else. Sina says no. Mrs. Hobbs says that if she finds any trace, "You'll be sorry."

Sina is now more frightened than ever. And Mrs. Hobbs returns to her old, abusive ways. Only now, the woman looks at Sina with an ominous, almost deadly, expression.

Sina returns to her childlike, frightened ways, like she was at the beginning. She returns to her old hairdo, clothing, and behavior.

Amy notices this too. She's worried at the sudden change. Amy confronts Sina, demanding to know what's happened.

With great reluctance, Sina tells her. Amy doesn't believe her and wants to see evidence. Sina says it's all gone, but that she wrote down her real parents' names, the name of the town, and the name of the newspaper.

Amy tells her father, and he calls the police. (**Key Pivotal Plot Point.**)

A detective, Ed Henton, forties, overweight and kind of dumpy. He comes out to talk to Amy and her dad. He points out that these are serious charges and that they're essentially hearsay from a woman considered to have limited intelligence.

Nevertheless, Detective Henton interviews Sina (without Mrs. Hobbs's knowledge). He takes a liking to her. (**Possible romantic subplot.**) He concludes that she's not stupid.

Because Detective Henton finds Sina appealing and because he feels sorry for her, he makes some calls and learns that the newspaper has long since gone out of business and the cops who worked on the case 35 years ago are all dead. And the files on the case were destroyed in a flood at the small town's police station. (**Complication.**)

He attempts to track down Will and Linda Tuttle. He hits a dead end. (**Complication.**) He reports this to Sina and says he's sorry. His affection for her is growing. He asks her out on a date. She can't believe it. She says no at first, but then yes. It's going to be secret.

But Mrs. Hobbs finds out (she inadvertently listened in on the phone extension) and is enraged, especially when she learns that Ed is a cop. (**Major Pivotal Plot Point.**) She demands to know how Sina met him, and because Sina's afraid of her, she blurts out that he was checking out the kidnapping.

Hearing this, Mrs. Hobbs knows that things are closing in. With Sina as the only witness who could testify against her, Mrs. Hobbs stares at Sina menacingly. She approaches her and smiles, saying that it's time they tried to heal all the wounds. They're going to do something fun together.

Meanwhile, Detective Henton gets a phone call from a cop in the town where the kidnapping took place. The caller has information that one of the investigating officers is still alive and living in a nursing home 100 miles away. (**Major Pivotal Plot Point resulting in further information being learned.**)

Detective Henton takes a shot and visits the guy. We meet retired Lieutenant Ray Paxton (who's in his eighties). He has good news and bad news. The bad news is that Will Tuttle died two years after the kidnapping and that Linda Tuttle moved away and passed on herself. He tells a story—perhaps we see it in flashback—about the primary suspect in the case.

She was a boarder living with Will and Linda Tuttle. She was a troublemaker, always picking fights, making noise, getting drunk, late with the rent. They told her to leave. The cops believed she took the Tuttles' baby to get even with them. He says that the woman had a distinctive birthmark on her right cheek and unusually large feet. (**Key exposition.**)

Detective Henton remembers noting that Marion Hobbs has big feet and a similar birthmark. He knows that she's the one. (**Major Pivotal Plot Point.**)

The good news Ray provides is that the Tuttles had another child—another *daughter*. Ray says he still exchanges Christmas cards with her. He even has her phone number. Detective Henton decides to surprise Sina with the news in person. He starts on the long drive home.

The next day. Amy observes Sina putting a picnic basket into her mother's car. Amy asks what's going on. Sina says that she and her mother are going on a picnic at a nearby lake and forest preserve.

Mrs. Hobbs comes out. She sees Amy, but instead of being her usual nasty self, she's friendly to Amy. Something doesn't seem right. Amy watches as they pull out. Sina looks out from the passenger side as they drive off.

Later. Amy's phone rings. It's Detective Henton. He tells Amy to tell Sina to sneak over to her house. He wants to tell her the good news. He also wants Sina out of the way because he's planning on arresting Mrs. Hobbs. Amy tells him that Sina and Mrs. Hobbs are gone and that they were going "to some lake for a picnic."

Detective Henton says there's only one place it could be. He takes off for the lake. Amy goes with him.

We join Sina and Mrs. Hobbs at the lake. It's manmade and in the midst of a dense forest preserve. They go to a secluded spot. As Sina is preparing for the picnic, Mrs. Hobbs is preparing for something else.

Detective Henton drives toward the lake. On the way he calls the police department for reinforcements. A couple of other cops in the small town respond.

Ultimately we build to a struggle between Sina and Mrs. Hobbs, culminating with Detective Henton and Amy arriving before the other cops.

Because Detective Henton is overweight, he moves slowly. Amy runs ahead and saves Sina by wrestling Mrs. Hobbs to the ground and holding her until Detective Henton gets there to make the arrest. Sina and Detective Henton hug each other. He kisses her. (**Romantic subplot takes off.**)

With Mrs. Hobbs under arrest and back to face the music for the kidnapping 35 years ago, Sina gets on with her life. (**Major Dramatic Question answered.**) Not only does she have Detective Henton and a great friend in Amy, she also has a sister.

Sina and Detective Henton are getting out of a car in front of a pleasant middle-class house. A woman resembling Sina but a few years younger, comes out of the house.

It's her sister, Barbara. She is happily married and has a couple of kids eager to meet and love their newfound aunt.

They embrace.

THE END

Nugget

How Long Should a Treatment Be?

Simply put, a treatment should be as long as it needs to be. It ends when you've gotten everything in. You'll understand this better after you've written one.

The Irony of Irony

*"Love is an ideal thing, marriage a real thing. Confusion of
the real with the ideal never goes unpunished."*

JOHANN WOLFGANG VON GOETHE

How often does something dramatic (good or bad, big or small)
happen to you? Something interesting enough to merit telling
someone about it?

For most of us, nothing out of the ordinary happens all that
often. For a few, something cathartic occurs. And often, dramatic
irony permeates that event.

A friend recounted how he had gone to a nightclub on the
Lower East Side. While there, someone had been killed in a knife
fight. In recounting the story, the dramatic experience was that my
friend was there and saw the person die. Frightening and interesting, but not ironic. At least not for him.

A few days later I happened to be talking to my mother in Ohio.
She casually mentioned that a guy who lived two blocks away from
her had been murdered in New York the previous weekend. Other
than the strangeness in hearing that someone from my old neighborhood—a person who had resided two blocks away from the
house I'd grown up in—had been murdered in New York, I
didn't pay much more attention. But then when my mother
read me the news story in the local paper, it dawned on me that
the murder victim was the same person my friend had seen die.

That's irony.

So much of life is filled with it. And so much of the irony of life is dramatic.

When I think of the irony I've experienced, observed, or shared with friends, it comes off like all the Shakespearean and Greek tragedies combined with the grit of a hard-boiled Raymond Chandler novel mixed in with the neurotic hysteria of Tennessee Williams.

In other words, it's been, well, *ironic*.

The following are examples of irony. They're all true. Some are serious, others amusing:

• The father of a friend of mine was a leader in his church and devoutly Catholic, considered by many to be the most religious man in town. He also had sex with his own daughters and even made one pregnant.

• The high-school girlfriend of a friend was the quintessential giddy, cloyingly childlike self-involved beauty. It was understood that she had never read a book in high school and hadn't read one in her adult life either. It was also understood that she didn't read the newspaper or pay attention to current events. Nevertheless, she went on to become a hugely successful real-estate agent making a six-figure salary. She's middle aged now, still gorgeous, dim-witted, and wealthy.

• A gay friend of mine loved to shock me with tales of his wild sexual behavior (prior to AIDS). He was into multiple partners, orgies, S&M, and the whole nine yards of sexual debauchery. But the time he shocked me most was his story of the guy he picked and *didn't* have sex with. All they did was kiss passionately for two hours. Just kissing. Some nuzzling on the neck. Some tonguing in the ear. Nothing else. He was 35 years old and had been active sexually since he was 15, but had never, literally, been kissed.

• I live in New York City, a place with perhaps a more visible homeless problem than most towns. Recently I moved. Moves in Manhattan often entail relocating only a few blocks away, but in a city as concentrated as New York, those few blocks might as well be 25 miles. I found different places to take dry cleaning, buy food, get a newspaper, and devised a new route to work. In my new neighborhood there were also new homeless people. Fine. In Manhattan you see these people and coexist. But one day, a few months after the move, I encountered one of the homeless men from my old neighborhood. He was going through a garbage can. I was walking my dog. Actually I spotted him at the exact time he saw me. There was a definite sense of recognition. I know he thought what I thought: *You're in a new neighborhood.* For a split second I almost said hello, but as I had never spoken to him in my old neighborhood, I decided against it now. Besides, what is there to say? The irony of this haunted me for weeks.

Make a list of the five most ironic things you've experienced directly or indirectly. You'll find that each one makes you sit back and think. And ponder. And maybe shake your head over how truly peculiar and sadly amusing life can be. All of which can be used in your screenplays.

Nugget

The Value of Old Movies

Movies from the 1930s and '40s are great lessons in screenwriting. They're strong on plot, they get started fast, and—*Citizen Kane* and *Gone With the Wind* notwithstanding—they were shorter back then. Turn on American Movie Classics or go to your video store and check out the running time of old films, both classics and the B movies. Most are less than 100 minutes. Some are less than 90 minutes. In the early days of Hollywood, screenwriters were up against censorship through the Hays Office, so they had to be less obvious and more clever. There's a lesson in this. It's easy to write clever X-rated edgy dialogue. It's hard to keep it clean but still be clever and hip.

The Single Bullet Theory of the JFK Assassination and How It Can Help the Plotting of Your Screenplay

"Lee Harvey Oswald acted alone."

CONCLUSION OF THE "WARREN REPORT"

I've always been a JFK assassination buff, a full-fledged card-carrying conspiracy theorist. I never felt Lee Harvey Oswald acted alone, and I always believed there was a second gunman.

But it wasn't until I saw Oliver Stone's *JFK* and watched the courtroom scene in which Kevin Costner as Prosecutor Jim Garrison diagrammed the trajectory of what became known as the Single Bullet Theory that it dawned on me that good writing has to be like that.

If you never saw the film or if you aren't entirely familiar with the Single Bullet Theory, it goes something like this:

There are those who are convinced that one bullet was responsible for the death of President Kennedy and the wounds received by Texas governor John Connally. According to this hypothesis, the same bullet that was fired into the back of JFK tumbled downward and to the right, managed to go through his chest, through Governor Connally's right shoulder, and into his right wrist.

Whether true or not, the underlying aspect of the theory is fascinating from a storytelling point of view.

The bullet's twists and turns are unpredictable. The presumption by most people, especially those of us who know nothing about guns and bullets, is that an ordinary bullet follows a linear path—like a script.

But the best screenplays (and all stories, for that matter) are those that throw us the proverbial curve ball, unexpected twist, unforeseen revelation, ingenious wrinkle, and unanticipated reversal.

In other words, it's fun to be fooled. It's fun to think a storyline is going in one direction only to find out it's going in another and that *that* direction is one that never even crossed your mind as a possibility. And when the writer is really clever, he tops that surprise with another. And another after that.

Make a list of five movies you've seen that genuinely surprised you with amazing plot turns, twists, and reversals. Then rent them. Then study them in the privacy of your own home.

Since you've already seen the films, you aren't watching them for enjoyment.

This is work.

An assignment.

Homework.

And even though this homework is watching a movie, it shouldn't be taken lightly. Don't watch it with anyone else. Sit in front of the screen by yourself with a pen and notebook.

Here's what to look for:

- The points in the film when you thought one thing was going to happen but something else did.
- The points in the film when something happened that came totally out of left field but was perfectly logical.
- The event in the last 10 minutes of the film that you never in a million years thought was coming.

- The event in the last 60 seconds of the film that you never expected.

The following five movies are filled with one outrageously clever twist and turn after another. Rent, study, and enjoy them too.

One Flew Over the Cuckoo's Nest, Psycho (the original), *The Deer Hunter, Waking Ned Devine,* and *Dave.*

Nugget

The 51st Girl

The most-used word in Hollywood is "no." It's short, easy to understand, and speaks volumes. It's easier to say than the three-letter word. It's also safer to live with than the three-letter word. The three-letter word is a commitment. Contracts have to be drawn up. Checks have to be written. Dozens of phone calls have to be made. Asses have to be put on the line. Who wants to put his ass and potentially his career on the line when a simple "no" will enable him to live and fight and, well, say "no" another day? You will hear the two-letter word more often than any other. Every screenwriter hears it, even the established, upper-echelon people. It's part of the package. You'll never like hearing it, but for your own peace of mind, get used to it. Just take it in and move on. Getting a "no" response to your screenplay is like a guy who asks out a girl. She says no. He finds another girl. Asks her. Again, no. He keeps asking and keeps getting told no.

He hits number 50. No. But then comes the 51st girl. She says, "Yes. I'd love to go out with you." Before the words are out of her mouth, he's forgotten the previous "no's" and he's concentrating on the "yes." This is how it is when you hear the three-letter word about your screenplay. All the two-letter words will evaporate into a quickly forgotten mist.

How Your Own "Wonder Years"
Will Provide Story Ideas
You Couldn't Imagine

"No one returns with good will to the place which has done him mischief."

PHAEDRUS

I'm one of those people blessed (or cursed, depending upon your point of view) with a flypaper mind that is a repository for tons of useless, meaningless details from my past.

Stuff like how I felt in first grade when I announced to the class that my sister has been born and no one cared. I remember crying and feeling bad because the only reason I'd brought it up was because another boy (I even remember his name) was singled out by the teacher (I don't remember her name) because his sister had just been born. Logic dictated to my six-year-old mind that if he was being singled out for having a new sister, so should I be. Wrong.

Now, I've got lots and lots of memories like this. Things that I wish I could forget. And from what most people tell me when I tell them about this memory of mine, they aren't like me. They've forgotten crap like this. The only good thing about this ability is that it opens up all kinds of windows to events from my youth that I can use.

When *The Wonder Years* appeared on television, it was an instant hit. I think it was successful because it captured so perfectly those giddy but painful adolescent years that we've all suffered through.

Here's a story from my own life. A friend of mine fixed me up with a girl for a blind date. Our only communication had been one telephone conversation during which I asked her to go to a dance at my high school—an all-boys Catholic school. The conversation was uneventful except for one piece of information she revealed. She hated guys who wore glasses.

Ouch! I wore glasses. Big ugly ones like Buddy Holly. No problem, I figured. I'll just take them off before I pick her up, then put them on when I drive, pointing out that I need them for driving. It made sense to me. It really did. And it worked too. Until we got to the dance.

What I hadn't counted on was the fact that everyone who knew me knew that I wore glasses. So when you're used to seeing someone with glasses not wearing them, you might tend to remark, "Where's your glasses?"

Which is what happened. After the sixth guy had remarked about the absence of my glasses, I could tell by the sneer on my date's face that she loathed me. We ended up leaving early. I took her home, and that was that. Pathetic, right? I was brimming with self-esteem, right? But it's fun to tell now. Actually it was kind of fun to tell a couple of days after it happened. But when I was living through it, I wanted to die of embarrassment.

Although back then I didn't know what a "character arc" was, I experienced one: Never lie about yourself to a woman. Is this a *Wonder Years* episode or what?

Here's another one.

Seventh grade. I had a crush on a girl, and at recess one day I made the mistake of telling a guy in the class my secret.

He promised he wouldn't tell the girl, who he happened to sit next to in class. Fifteen minutes later, as the class was filtering back into the classroom, I happened to turn around and overhear the kid say to the girl, "Guess who likes you?" To which she replied, with a grotesque grimace, "Eewwwwwoooo."

I was devastated. And I immediately stopped liking her.

Jump ahead five years. I'm a senior in high school attending an all-boys Catholic school. Near my house was the local public high school. I'm walking down a street, and I see a car pull up. Two guys and a girl are in the car. The car stops and the passenger door flies open.

I hear a guy yell, "Get the Hell out, you whore." And who do I see scrambling out of the car but the girl in my seventh-grade class who was so unimpressed that I liked her.

Our eyes met. We hadn't seen each other since eighth grade. She recognized me. I remember the moment as if it were yesterday. We didn't acknowledge each other. She was still clearly upset and embarrassed at being called a whore by the guys who kicked her out of the car.

I kept walking. I was secretly glad. But I also felt a tinge of compassion for her. Very slight.

The point of these two anecdotes is that they're both small events in my life that were powerful enough to affect me. They were little movies with beginnings, middles, and endings. And over the years I've related them in classrooms or to friends sharing their adolescent war stories.

I know you have a few. Some might be as fresh in your memory as if they happened yesterday. Others might be only a thin haze in your mind. Think hard. Remember the pain or embarrassment. Write down every detail. You might laugh about it now—and there just might be a movie in it.

Nugget

Everybody Needs Somebody
Sometime

No one succeeds on his or her own. Sure, some get a head start because they're born wealthy or into a family with connections. There's an understanding that, once they're ready to begin a career, phone calls will be made and jobs will be gotten whether they're qualified or not. Others make their own connections: the internship or part-time job that leads to something. School ties help some get their foot in the door. Dating the right person is another way in. Then there are the rest of us who don't know a soul, go to the wrong schools, join the wrong clubs (if we join anything at all). We're lousy at networking and schmoozing because we're shy, unassertive, or socially inept. We have greater odds against succeeding and consequently, from a dramatic point of view, are more interesting to watch. Same with a movie. The wealthy or connected person and the unconnected regular guy will handle the same problem differently. One can call his dad or frat brother or whomever. The regular Joe can't call anybody. He's on his own as he tries to resolve his crisis. Now, in the real world he'll most likely get totally screwed and wind up crashing and burning unless he gets someone to help him. In a screenplay, help comes from allies and mentors. These are the individuals who pop in and out of your story offering advice, guidance, and wisdom. The value of allies and mentors in storytelling is incalculable.

CHAPTER 20

And Then What?

"By a small sample we may judge of the whole piece."

MIGUEL DE CERVANTES

An idea that isn't quite there stinks like a dead fish.

Unfortunately everybody knows it but you. It's kind of like the wife of the philandering husband being the last to find out her mate is sleeping with his secretary, the church organist, and half of her bowling team.

I've heard enough students pitch ideas for scripts they want to write and I've pitched enough of my own to hear the three most dreaded words: *And then what?*

"And then what?" is the response of someone (producer, development person, friend, parent, child) who has listened to you talk out your new storyline only to get a blank, sympathetic, or confused stare that says you haven't piqued their interest, or worse, that you've lost them, or even worse, that you've bored them.

The problem with having "And then what?" asked of you is that it makes you look bad. Amateurish. Like you haven't done your homework or weren't professional enough to have spent the time getting your story down.

How do you avoid hearing these words? Make sure you've thought your story through. Know where all the Pivotal Plot Points come. Know where the act breaks fall. Know what your main character wants. Have a clear idea of how the story will end.

And then what?

Practice talking out your story to yourself. Out loud. Sit in front of a mirror and talk. Get used to hearing your own voice.

And then what?

You'll be ready to do it for real.

And then what?

You'll sound like someone who has prepared.

And then what?

Maybe, just maybe, the person you tell it to will say the sweetest words a screenwriter can hear: "I like it."

Nugget

The Bio-Pic

You want to write a movie about the life of someone famous. The hardest obstacle you'll face is where to start. From the moment of birth? After death? At the pinnacle of a career? It's not as easy as you might think to figure out where to begin. The movie version of Howard Stern's *Private Parts* is a flawless piece of biographical screenwriting by Len Blum and Michael Kalesniko. It began not at a high moment in Stern's career but at one of the lowest: his appearance as his alter ego Fartman at the MTV Music Video Awards show. He did his thing, went backstage, and was ostracized by the rock stars hanging in the wings. Howard's own voiceover quickly takes us back to him as a child, where we meet his parents and get a taste of his early years. From that moment on it was a point-by-point chronology of his rise to fame, filled with setbacks and ultimate success. It also chronicled the love story between Stern and his wife, which added another dimension to his life. The film did not end with Howard winding up as the best-selling author of *Private Parts* and self-proclaimed King of All Media that he was to become. It ended before he achieved national prominence. He had won over the New York market. The rest of the country was to follow. This was a smart move by the filmmakers. They ended it at the first pinnacle of Stern's success. And they left his fans wanting more.

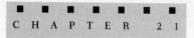

The Completed Process:
Vague Idea to Basic Premise to
Three-Act Storyline to Screenplay

*"And now I have finished a work that neither the wrath of
love, nor fire, nor the sword, nor devouring age shall be able
to destroy."*

OVID

What follows is the actual process I needed to write a screenplay
called *Living Proof*. It literally began with the Vague Idea of "What
would've happened if the last American astronauts on the Moon
found a crashed UFO?"

I expanded that by a few lines, then into a three-act storyline,
and then into a 117-page screenplay of which I've included the
first 15 pages.

The most important point I want to make is that I wrote four
drafts of the screenplay, and before I finished the first draft I completely discarded Act Three of the original storyline.

VAGUE IDEA

The last team of astronauts on the Moon finds a crashed UFO and alien
remains.

BASIC PREMISE

A U.S. astronaut from the early '70s Apollo space program learns that he's dying. He decides to come forward with information about what he and two other astronauts discovered on the Moon but were ordered to remain silent about—specifically, the presence of humanlike remains and a crashed spaceship that's clearly not from Earth. He contacts one of the surviving astronauts and asks him to come forth too, but this guy says no for fear of losing his reputation; he's a popular congressman. When the first astronaut dies mysteriously, the other one decides to risk his career and life to bring the truth to the American people. But before he can do this, he is discredited and hunted down by the Air Force. To save his career and life, he must find the only existing evidence of what he saw before the government does.

THREE-ACT STORYLINE

ACT ONE

Congressman Tyler Banks, former astronaut famous for the last landing on the Moon, is at the peak of his life and career. He's in his early fifties but looks much younger and has just won his seventh congressional term. He wrote a bestseller about being an astronaut, and he's a popular guest on talk shows, known for his wit and humor. He's also one of the most eligible bachelors in Washington.

After we see Tyler in his world, we can't help but feel that, although he's a good man and popular guy, he has one flaw: He plays it safe politically. But he's so damn charming and likable.

Tyler's comfortable world comes crashing down when he is paid a visit by Brody Pierson, one of his fellow astronauts on the Moon mission. Brody, a good ole boy from Texas who's spent his post-astronaut years as a college professor, tells Tyler he is dying and that he wants to go public with what they saw when they were on the Moon nearly 30 years before: specifically, the remains of humanlike beings and a crashed spaceship not from Earth.

Tyler is against going public, reminding Brody that they were sworn never to discuss what they saw, in the interest of national security. But Brody says that was a lifetime ago and it's time for the truth to be told. He begs Tyler to stand by his side and back him up. But Tyler declines, primarily because he always plays it safe. He feels that to do this would be political suicide.

Brody leaves. He then visits the *third* astronaut on the Moon trip (Hal Buford), but this guy is a victim of premature Alzheimer's. He lives with his 35-year-old daughter and her 10-year-old son. Brody realizes that Hal will be of no help to him.

So Brody decides to go it alone. He calls a press conference and reveals what he, Tyler, and Hal saw. Spin control by the Air Force immediately denounces what he's said as the remarks of a delusional man trying to gain one last moment in the sun before dying.

Of course, the highest-ranking Air Force guy in charge (Yale Rooker) knows it's true, and he contacts Tyler. We learn that Yale Rooker has known about what the astronauts saw from the start and that he now heads up the Air Force cover-up and disinformation on all UFO activity.

Yale orders Tyler to publicly denounce Brody. Again, we see his character flaw in action. Reluctantly, Tyler appears on TV and totally contradicts everything Brody said.

Brody, realizing that Tyler's denouncement is the kiss of death, calls him and tells him off.

Then Brody expands on something he said at the press conference: There is actual film footage of the crashed spaceship and alien remains. Tyler knows about the footage, saying that it's in a secret vault in Washington. But what Tyler *didn't* know is that Hal, the Alzheimer astronaut, who took pictures of the crash, kept one of the reels and held on to it after they were sworn to secrecy. The problem is that with the passage of so many years and with Hal having no memory, Brody doesn't know where the secret reel is.

Brody says that he's going to devote whatever time he has left to finding the footage. And when he does, he's going to expose it and Tyler for lying and being a moral coward.

Tyler finds himself in a bind: If the missing footage is found by Brody, exposing it will destroy Tyler's image and reputation. If the Air Force gets it, they'll hide it with the other footage, and Tyler's career will be fine.

So Tyler, still playing politics and still following the oath he took 30 years ago to remain silent about the discovery on the Moon, decides to stay on the side of the Air Force.

Feeling he is doing the right thing, he tells Yale Rooker about the secret reel of footage.

Then Brody is murdered. Only it doesn't look like a murder. It looks like a suicide. But Tyler's not so sure. He knew that Brody was deeply religious and that he would never take his own life.

ACT TWO

Tyler suspects something is wrong, but he goes on with his life. Only now, wherever he is, people ask him questions about the spaceship on the Moon. He can't get away from it.

Then the Alzheimer astronaut dies. Tyler goes to the funeral. The daughter (Lauren, 35) and her son (Walt, 10) are friendly toward Tyler. Lauren admits that her father's death was a relief. It was difficult caring for him and he was out of it and in pain.

We learn that Tyler didn't keep in touch with Hal and hadn't seen Lauren since she was a kid. She admits to having a huge crush on Tyler when she was 5. And now Tyler can't help but have a crush on her. So begins a romantic subplot.

Lauren brings up Brody's death and the press conference he held. She admits to thinking that Brody must have been losing his mind, adding that "Daddy never said a word about any crashed spaceship and bodies to me."

But then, little Walt casually remarks, "Grampa told me all about it."

Hearing this, Lauren laughs it off and tells Walt to stop telling lies. Tyler knows the kid is telling the truth. Then Lauren says two men from the Air Force visited her father a week before he died, asking him questions about what he saw on the Moon. She adds that because of the Alzheimer's her father wasn't much help.

When Lauren leaves to get some refreshments, Tyler asks Walt a question: "What did your grandfather tell you he saw on the Moon?"

Walt says that Grandpa Hal drew him a picture. Walt shows him a rough drawing of the Moon landscape, a crashed spaceship, and several bodies in human form.

Tyler then asks if Grandpa Hal told him about a movie showing what he'd seen. Walt says yes, but that it's in a safe place. Tyler pushes for more information, but all the kid says is that his grandfather told him that someday men might come and ask him about the footage, and he should never tell anyone where it is unless he trusts them.

Tyler asks Walt if he trusts him. Walt says not yet.

Meanwhile, ever the loyal soldier, Tyler reports back to Yale with this information.

Tyler also finds himself wanting to see Lauren, so he calls her up for a date. She accepts. It's pleasant. Tyler pushes her to find out more of what her father might have said, and it's clear that she knows nothing. She explains that Hal and Walt developed a special bond after her marriage ended. Hal became more of a father than a grandfather.

They arrive home from their date only to find the babysitter hysterical and an ambulance taking Walt to the hospital, where he remains in a coma.

Tyler's convinced that Yale is trying to silence everyone connected to the astronauts. He knows that the only ones left are Lauren and himself.

He knows that if the Air Force will try to kill a kid, they'll stop at nothing.

Now more than ever, he must find the secret footage, and he knows that the only link to it is little Walt. But with Walt in a coma, he has nowhere to turn.

Tyler feels the only hope is Lauren. Maybe she can remember something her father said . . . some overheard bit of conversation . . . something whispered . . . something that seemed like nothing but might be important.

Lauren can't remember anything significant. As she recounts her father's and Walt's relationship, she simplifies it by saying that they did mainly two things together: read books and watch movies, specifically sci-fi films and stories set in outer space. They videotaped everything, and together they were building quite a film library.

This eventually leads to a break. While at Lauren's house, Tyler is checking through Hal's personal effects. He finds nothing. He stumbles onto the film library that Walt and Hal have created. There are hundreds of cassettes alphabetized by genre. Tyler casually checks some of the titles out.

Now, to cut to the chase: One of the titles doesn't seem right. Tyler puts it in the VCR. It's the actual footage of the crash and alien bodies.

He shows it to Lauren. She's dumbfounded. With the reel in his possession, Tyler is ready to do the right thing and go public in honor of his murdered partners, Brody and Hal.

ACT THREE

Tyler tries to organize a press conference, but there's a new problem. Yale and the Air Force bad guys have put out new spin control.

They're claiming that *Tyler* murdered Brody and almost killed Walt.

While Tyler and Lauren are hiding from the authorities, she asks why they had to keep the crashed ship and bodies secret. Tyler explains that the Vietnam War was in full gear. The Cold War was at its peak. The country was in turmoil. It wasn't the right time to tell the people about life on other planets.

Meanwhile, as the authorities are closing in on Tyler, he realizes that a public press conference would be too visible. He might be assassinated. He tries to figure out a way to get the footage shown.

An idea hits him. In an early scene in the film, we'll show Tyler meeting with a lobbyist for a new cable news network à la MSNBC that's trying to get licensed in larger cities. The lobbyist has been wining and dining Tyler, and he keeps saying no. But now Tyler contacts the guy with an idea.

They meet. The guy shows the tape on his news network, and then the bigger news stations pick it up. In short, the world has seen the crashed spaceship and remains.

The Air Force has to come up with some fast spin control. They bring in experts who disclaim the footage as fake. Tyler, Brody, and Hal are all criticized. A story is made up that the bodies and crash they saw were planted to test their veracity. The skeptics and believers clash. People don't know who to believe, so they believe what they want.

Tyler feels his reputation is shattered. He realizes there's only one way to prove he, Brody, and Hal were right, and that's by going back to the Moon.

He calls in the chips on all his connections, both political and military, and finagles a ride on one of the lunar probes that are regularly launched.

The story ends with Tyler and the small crew he's with landing on the Moon in the same place where he landed 30 years before.

Sure enough, the crashed spaceship and remains are still there. Tyler is vindicated. Upon his return, Walt comes out of his coma, it's clear that Lauren and Tyler will be an item, and he's more popular than ever.

THE END

LIVING PROOF

(First 15 pages of the screenplay)

FADE IN ON

Footage of the first Moon landing, July 20, 1969, showing Neil Armstrong stepping onto the Moon surface.

NEIL ARMSTRONG

That's one small step for man and one giant step for mankind.

WIDEN TO REVEAL—A NEWSCASTER

In CNN's Washington, D.C., bureau. In the background, more footage of the first Moon landing rolls. The astronauts hit golf balls, jump up and down, etc.

NEWSCASTER

Twenty-one days and counting until men will again be walking on the Moon. But when NASA announced plans to go back to the Moon earlier this year, not everyone was pleased. Ironically one of the most visible and loudest critics of the forthcoming Moon launch is none other than the last man to walk on the Moon—Tyler Banks, now a senator from Pennsylvania. Welcome!

CLOSE ON TYLER BANKS

Fit, handsome, and vibrant, looking younger than a man in his early fifties. He wears a well-tailored suit and an unusually garish tie.

NEWSCASTER

NASA shut down the Apollo program in 1974, shortly after you, Brody Pierson, and Hal Buford returned from the Moon. One would think you would be more supportive of NASA's renewed interest in the Moon.

TYLER

Frankly, I don't believe the Moon is where we should be directing our efforts in the twenty-first century. What's that expression? "Been there, done that?"

NEWSCASTER

Why did we stop going to the Moon in the first place?

TYLER

Because we got what we went there for.

NEWSCASTER

To beat the Russians?

TYLER

That was the initial plan. Once we did that, it was all about science. Mainly the moon rocks. They were all our scientists needed to start their research. But they've learned everything there is to know. The new crew going up there won't find anything fresh except maybe the footprints of all the astronauts who came before.

NEWSCASTER

Then what does NASA hope to achieve from going back?

TYLER

Wouldn't surprise me if a couple of hotshot real-estate developers were interested in selling time shares.

The newscaster and Tyler share a laugh.

TYLER (cont'd)

Personally I think we already know all the Moon's secrets.

NEWSCASTER

John Glenn asked to go back into space. Is there a small part of you that wishes you could go back to the Moon?

TYLER

The only place I want to get back to is Washington in the next election. There's nothing on the Moon I want to see.

MALE VOICE (off-screen)

Once was enough.

Suddenly the sound is muted. Tyler and the newscaster keep talking, but we don't hear them.

PULL BACK TO REVEAL that we are in—SOMEONE'S DEN

It's a virtual shrine to the U.S. space program. Photos of rockets, launches, and astronauts from the '60s looking cocky and fit with their crewcuts. Presidents from Kennedy to Nixon posing with astronauts from the various missions, numerous shots of the Moon, *Time* magazine covers.

CLOSE ON—A FRAMED NEWSPAPER HEADLINE:

APOLLO 18 MARKS LAST FLIGHT TO THE MOON

CLOSE ON—ONE PHOTOGRAPH OF THREE YOUNG ASTRONAUTS, circa 1974

One is Tyler. The other two are BRODY PIERSON and HAL BUFORD, his Apollo crew.

ANGLE—BRODY PIERSON NOW

Age 58. Sunken eyes. Pale skin. This man is not well. He looks at Tyler's face on the TV screen.

BRODY

(Southern accent)

Time to tell the truth, ole buddy.

Brody's wife, SYLVIA, 53, sits next to him.

SYLVIA

The truth about what, Brody?

Brody looks at her, says nothing.

EXT. TYLER'S CONDO IN WASHINGTON—NIGHT

Masculine and tasteful. The furniture is very Ethan Allen. Solid and reliable, like the man who lives here. There is a noticeable lack of a woman's touch.

There's a magnificent view of the Washington skyline. Tyler is checking the messages on his answering machine.

> TYLER'S DAUGHTER'S VOICE
>
> Hi, Daddy, you were great on the news tonight. But, my God, where did you find that tie? Love ya.

Tyler smiles as he looks at his tie.

> BRODY'S VOICE
>
> It's Brody. Caught your "act" on the tube. Still playin' the game, eh? Who told you what to say? I'm flyin' in to Washington tomorrow. I'll swing by your office.

Tyler glances at a framed photograph of himself and Brody as young astronauts. He smiles.

> YALE ROOKER'S VOICE
> (ominous-sounding)
>
> You were being too nice again. Like last week on *Meet the Press*. I want more negativity. More about how irresponsible NASA is being. And I didn't like that stuff about the Moon's "secrets." Call me.

Tyler looks concerned. He speed-dials a number.

> YALE ROOKER (off-screen)
>
> Yes?

INTERCUT

INT. YALE ROOKER'S OFFICE—NIGHT

COLONEL YALE ROOKER, late '60s. Looks meaner than any drill sergeant who has ever lived. Dressed in uniform. Air Force. Smoking a pipe. A row of surveillance screens is on one wall. Various magazines and newspapers with headlines and stories about the new Moon launch are spread out on his desk. All are critical of the launch. There are two phones on his desk. One normal-looking, the other off to the side and a different shape and color. *That's* the one he's talking on.

> **TYLER**
>
> It's Tyler. How can you say I wasn't critical enough? I spent the entire interview dumping on NASA.

> **YALE**
>
> I'm taking the gloves off for the next three weeks. I have articles hostile to the launch coming out in five magazines and seven newspapers. Our Web page is getting a thousand hits a day. If we can create enough of a groundswell, we can stop this goddamn thing. What else? Ah. I'm lining up a spot for you on *Politically Incorrect*. By the way, where the Hell did you get that tie?

> (hangs up)

Tyler looks at his tie.
INT. 747—DAY
Brody sits in a window seat. Spread around him are several newspapers including *The New York Times, Houston Chronicle, USA Today,* etc. He has cut out several articles about the forthcoming Moon launch. A laptop computer rests on the serving tray. On the screen the following sentences appear—
INSERT—Ladies and gentlemen, 25 years ago I walked on the Moon, and today I am finally going to reveal what I saw. After returning from the Moon, three young astronauts took

an oath to lie. When your country asks you to lie in the interest of national security, you do it without question.

But a lingering doubt remains.

Brody looks out the window. Thinks. Starts to write again.

EXT. CONGRESSIONAL OFFICE BUILDING, WASHINGTON, D.C.—DAY

Lots of marble, granite, and stairs. Huge. Imposing. Power hangs in the air. Tourists taking pictures blend in with hustling congressional aides, lobbyists, protesters, and homeless people. One crazed-looking homeless man babbles about aliens colonizing the Moon.

INT. CORRIDOR—DAY

High ceilings. Large windows. The hundred-year-old building reeks of history. The hustle and bustle of powerful people in a hurry permeates the place. Tyler walks briskly down the corridor listening to his chief of staff, TOM RINNELLI, 30-ish, hyper, and nursing an ulcer.

> TOM
>
> You have a photo-op at five with a nun who stopped a bank robbery.

> TYLER
>
> Don't tell me she was armed.

> TOM
>
> She poked the guy in the eye with her rosary. You're giving her a medal. It'll look good for the folks back home. Then you meet with George Gimborzini.

> TYLER
>
> Why do I know that name?

TOM

He's the Ted Turner wannabe who's been trying to kiss your butt for a year. I think it's time to let him pucker up. He's got deep pockets.

TYLER

Anything else?

TOM

Newsweek wants to do a cover on the new astronaut team for the Moon shot with you and your team.

TYLER

I want to play that down.

TOM

Why? You're down in the polls. This new Moon shot is a plum. It's worth millions of dollars in publicity.

TYLER

That's old news. Besides, I hate *Newsweek*. They accused me of wearing a hairpiece.

They enter a door that leads into Tyler's outer office.
INT. TYLER'S OUTER OFFICE AREA—DAY
Impressive. Traditional mahogany desks. Lots of elegant wood paneling. His primary staff is located here. Interns are at the photocopy machine or on phones. It's a busy place. Tyler and Tom approach Tyler's secretary, MARY.

MARY

There's an astronaut in your office. He said you're expecting him.

TYLER

Brody!

MARY

Senator, this is none of my business, but when's the last time you saw him?

TYLER

Couple years. Why?

MARY

He doesn't look well.

Tyler takes in the comment, then steps into his office.

INT. TYLER'S OFFICE—DAY

Much like his apartment. Classic oxblood leather sofa and chairs. Gorgeous cherrywood desk. Stiffel lamps. A small terrace provides an impressive overlook of Washington. Besides the usual political pictures and stuff, there's a wall of astronaut and space-related photos. Tyler enters and notices Brody looking at a large photo of them in astronaut gear. Tyler can't help but notice how unhealthy Brody looks. He barely hides his concern. Tyler stands next to Brody and looks at the photo.

TYLER

That was a lifetime ago.

BRODY

Seems like yesterday to me. But then I always did live in the past.

TYLER

You've lost a little weight.

BRODY

Actually I lost a lot. Thirty-two pounds to be exact. Started dropping off a couple months ago. I have cancer. Of the pancreas. Yesterday the quack I go to gives me three months.

TYLER
(visibly upset)

Bullshit. We'll get a second opinion. I'll call the Mayo Clinic and have you checked in by morning.

Tyler grabs the telephone.

TYLER (cont'd)

Buddy of mine's in charge. He owes me big. I got his son into Harvard. Kid barely has the brains to make fries at Burger King.

BRODY

Put the phone down. It's too late for me. I had a great life. Hell, I got to walk on the Moon.

TYLER

What brings you to town?

BRODY

I'm gonna go public about what we saw on the Moon.

Tyler is stunned.

TYLER

Brody, that's top-secret classified information. *Above* top-secret. We took an oath.

BRODY

They forced us to take it.

TYLER

Nobody forced me to do anything. I did what my country asked me to do.

BRODY

They asked you to lie. Us. I don't want to go out lying. And now that NASA's sending guys back to the Moon, they'll find out anyway.

Brody coughs, takes out a handkerchief.

BRODY (cont'd)

I want to hold a press conference. I'd like you and Hal to stand by my side. The three of us could put on a pretty good dog and pony show.

TYLER

Obviously you haven't seen Hal recently. He has Alzheimer's. His daughter and her son moved to Virginia last year to care for him. I saw him six months ago. He didn't know me. Don't count on him remembering what we saw.

BRODY

Then it'll be you and me.

TYLER

Brody, have you thought about the consequences of doing this? Have you told anyone?

BRODY

Not a soul. Not even Sylvia. Married twenty-nine years and it's the only thing I ever kept from her. Tyler, I'm asking you to do this with me as my dying wish.

TYLER
(clearly torn)

Brody, we have a duty to . . .

BRODY

I feel a duty to tell the world what we saw on the Moon.

Tyler stares at Brody, then steps out onto the terrace. The Capitol glows in the distance.

EXT. TERRACE – DAY

Brody follows Tyler onto the terrace.

> TYLER
>
> Even if I agreed to do it, there's no proof. Without some-thing tangible, the media will laugh us out of town.
>
> (beat)
>
> And if that's not bad enough, Yale Rooker and his disinfor-mation people will destroy us. You'd be portrayed as a bit-ter fool looking for one last moment in the sun. And they'd say I'm using it as an election-year stunt.

> BRODY
>
> There is proof.

The sentence hangs in the air.

> TYLER
>
> What?

> BRODY
>
> There's a reel of film.

> TYLER
>
> We turned that in the minute we got back.

> BRODY
>
> Not that. There's *another* reel of film. Hal took it. He never turned it in.

> TYLER
>
> Why do you know about it and not me?

BRODY

Maybe because Hal knew you'd take your oath more seri-
ously than us.

TYLER

(stung by the remark)

Do you have it?

BRODY

No. Hal hid it. Where, I don't know.

TYLER

His mind's gone. He won't remember what he did with it.
Without that reel of film, it'd just be words. Forget about
it, Brody.

Brody mulls this over for a moment.

BRODY

Then I'll have to find it. And when I do, with you or without you, I'm gonna talk.

Brody turns and walks away. Tyler looks pensive.

INT. CLASSY RESTAURANT—NIGHT

An elegant bistro where powerful people get wined and dined.
Chandeliers. Tiffany lamps. Fine crystal and china. A pianist
plays classical music. Waiters wear tuxedos. Tyler and his
aide, Tom, sit with the previously mentioned Ted Turner
wannabe, GEORGE GIMBORZINI, 35. Long black hair, 300
pounds. He could easily be mistaken for a mobster. He eats a
huge steak. He chews as he talks. It's not pretty.

Tyler looks preoccupied and bored as George talks. Tyler
glances out the window and there it is—

TYLER'S P.O.V.—THE FULL MOON

But it's a hazy night and clouds drift in front of the Moon like a wispy veil.

>   **GIMBORZINI**
>   (butters some bread)

Ted Turner deserves all the credit in the world for creating CNN back in the '80s, but he doesn't deserve all the money. Whatever happened to good old American competition? But there can't be any competition when cable systems are afraid to say no to CNN.

(sets fork down)

All I ask is for your support during the next FCC vote. And I'm prepared to reciprocate your kindness with a substantial contribution to your campaign fund.

>   **TOM**

We appreciate that enormously.

Tom nudges Tyler. He looks away from the Moon.

>   **TYLER**

Uh . . . right. Enormously.

INT. TYLER'S APARTMENT—NIGHT

Tyler is stretched out on his couch, deep in thought, nursing a Scotch and water. *The Washington Post* is on his lap, turned to a story critical of the new Moon launch. Tyler glances at three framed photographs on an end table: Tyler and his late wife, Tyler and his daughter, and Tyler, Brody, and Hal in civilian clothes meeting Richard Nixon.

Suddenly he grabs the phone and speed-dials a number.

EXT. THE PENTAGON—NIGHT

An aerial shot. Slo-Mo. We fly over the Pentagon. And we keep going past all the "power buildings" and into—
GEORGETOWN
Specifically camera comes to rest on a quaint, harmless-looking townhouse on a residential street. A simple brass plaque over the doorbell reads PRIVATE CLUB.
INT. TOWNHOUSE—NIGHT
Only it doesn't look like an elegant townhouse should. There is no expansive foyer or parlor or winding staircase. Instead the insides of this townhouse have been gutted and transformed into a high-tech office filled with state-of-the-art computers and communication equipment. This is a *satellite operation* of NASA. It exists within the Air Force, Department of Defense.
INT. YALE ROOKER'S OFFICE IN THE TOWNHOUSE—NIGHT
Yale is at the computer by his desk, hammering out an article critical of the new Moon launch.
The unusual-looking phone rings. He answers it.

                    YALE
     Yes?

                    TYLER
     It's Tyler. Figured I'd find you at the office. Old worka-
     holics never go home. They just keep finding things to do
     to piss normal people off.

                    YALE
     You're not supposed to call on this line unless it's a matter
     of national security.

                    TYLER
     Does Project Magellan qualify as national security?

Yale perks up, looking alarmed.

> YALE

Spit it out.

> TYLER

Brody Pierson is going to go public.

> YALE

No one will believe him.

> TYLER

He wants me to do it with him.

> YALE

I don't blame him. Having a United States senator will look good. But without any proof, there's nothing.

> TYLER

Brody seems to think there is proof.

> YALE

Bullshit.

> TYLER

He says Hal Buford has a reel of film. Something he kept secret from everyone.

> YALE

Did you know about it?

> TYLER

No.

> YALE

How soon can you get here?

TYLER

I'm on my way.

Yale hangs up. Thinks for a moment. Looks concerned. He gets up and crosses to a large file cabinet. He reaches for a key and opens it. He sifts through several color-coded files, then comes to an inch-thick red file— Project Magellan. He returns to his desk. Dials the phone.

YALE

Project Magellan has just turned active again. My office.

(he hangs up)

INT. YALE'S OFFICE—NIGHT

20 minutes later. Tyler sits across from Yale. The Project Magellan file is on the desk.

YALE

Should I assume that Hal has this reel of film?

TYLER

I guess. But since he has Alzheimer's, there's a high probability he won't remember where it is.

YALE

Then my people will find it. Without that footage, Brody'll come off like some UFO nut.

TYLER

Yale, he wants to clear his conscience. He just found out he's dying.

YALE

Oh?

TYLER

He figures that the new astronauts will find what we saw, so why keep the secret any longer? He may have a point.

YALE

Nobody's gonna "find" anything.

TYLER

Why not?

YALE

Don't give it another thought. Thanks for bringing it to my attention.

TYLER

Has what we saw on the Moon been removed?

YALE

Yes. Now, leave it alone. Here's what I need you to do. Talk to Brody. Remind him that breaking the oath is treason. He'll be arrested.

TYLER

He won't care. He has three months to live.

YALE

Warn Brody that if he holds a press conference there will be *another* press conference held by you. You will denounce him as a sad, pathetic case emotionally disturbed because of his terminal illness.

TYLER

It won't work. When Brody sets his mind to something, he doesn't budge.

YALE

Brody will most certainly budge. One way or another. Your way or mine. My way will be a lot more painful.

TYLER

What are you saying, Yale?

YALE

If your friend wants to enjoy the last few months of his life, tell him to deep-six his little agenda.

TYLER

That sounds pretty ominous.

YALE

As well it should.

TYLER

All you've ever asked me to do is keep a secret and periodically bad-mouth NASA. Now you're sounding like a mob boss planning a hit.

(beat)

Give me some truth, Yale.

YALE

I can't. Even if I wanted to. Evidently you haven't heard that I'm retiring at the end of the year. I'm training my replacement.

TYLER

Who is he?

                          YALE

It's not a he. It's a she.

(waves to someone behind Tyler)

Here she is now.

Tyler turns around and sees a woman in the doorway—
HAZEL SINCLAIR, 35. Icy. No-nonsense. Intense. Very
smart. Education: Harvard, M.I.T., FBI Academy. Dressed in
a tasteful business suit. Looks like a $300,000-a-year invest-
ment banker.

                          YALE

Glad you could join us, Hazel.

She extends her right hand to Tyler, smiles respectfully.

                         HAZEL

Senator Banks, Hazel Sinclair. It's an honor to meet you.
My father was a great admirer of yours. Before I found my
chosen field, I wanted to be an astronaut, largely because
of you.

(she sits)

                         TYLER

How did you decide that working in Air Force disinformation was your chosen field?

                         HAZEL

Being on Earth was less frightening than space. So, what's
going on with Project Magellan?

                          YALE

The Senator here wants to know more.

HAZEL

How much more?

TYLER

If you expect me to go on national TV and betray, not to mention humiliate, one of my oldest friends, there better be one colossal reason why.

YALE

It's always better to betray a friend than your country. Friends can be replaced. Your country can't.

TYLER

Tell me what's going down or I'll be standing next to Brody on the Capitol steps.

YALE

For twenty-five years you've done what I told you, and you never asked questions.

TYLER

Maybe I should've.

YALE

To know more means even greater secrecy. And responsibility.

TYLER

I'm ready for it.

HAZEL

And ruthlessness.

YALE

Yes. Are you ready for the ruthlessness?

> TYLER

I'm ready to do whatever it takes to uphold the safety of my country.

> YALE

You think so? Tell you what. I'll make a deal with you. If you can convince Brody not to hold his press conference and to go quietly back to Houston . . . I'll get you a security-clearance upgrade.

> TYLER

Deal.

One hundred and two pages later, my initial Vague Idea resulted in a completed script. From first draft to final draft, eight months.

PART 2

Characterization

■ ■ ■ ■ ■ ■ ■ ■ ■

"Truth does not blush."

QUINTUS SEPTIMIUS TERTULLIAN

Getting Reacquainted With Who You Are and Where You've Been

"Strong reasons make strong actions."

WILLIAM SHAKESPEARE

Which comes first, the chicken or the egg?

Here's a tougher question: Which comes first, character or plot?

It depends.

Some people come up with a dynamite story that can be plotted out fairly simply. Their particular Hell will be in creating an interesting protagonist.

Others don't have the foggiest notion of a storyline but have an intriguing main character. Finding the right plot to put this character in will be what keeps them up nights screaming.

Given my druthers, I'd rather have the story and worry about a protagonist later simply because it's easier to construct a character than a storyline.

Easier. Hah!

Let me get something out in the open: Whenever I describe something as being "easier," I don't mean that literally. From this moment on, when I use the word *easier,* I really mean "slightly less difficult."

Constructing a character is looking first at yourself, then at everybody else. The best way to look at yourself is to get in touch with the less than flattering sides to your personality.

Why?

I know that Mother Teresa was kind, loving, and charitable to everyone she encountered. A true saint on Earth. But that's not dramatic. It's just, well, nice. It would be more interesting to know that she was a closet fan of *Melrose Place,* relaxed by reading Tom Clancy novels, and liked to pig out on Ring-Dings.

Answering the following questions will help you get reacquainted with who you are and where you've been. Try writing your answers in longhand rather than typing them. You'll take more time to think them through. I encourage you to be brutally honest.

1. What is the worst thing that ever happened to you?
2. What are the three biggest regrets of your life?
3. Who or what would you die for?
4. What is the worst thing you've ever done?
5. Who are you prejudiced against?

You might be wondering how the answers to any or all of these questions will help you start a screenplay. Welcome to the world of character development. The first character you're going to "develop" is you.

Let's use Question One as an example.

Did the worst thing that ever happened to you come to mind instantly, or did you have to think about it? Did you have a hard time pinpointing only one event? Were there two or three things (or more) that could qualify as "worst"? Did digging into such painful territory make you ill at ease? Did you remember something you had blocked out for years? Did something you previously thought of as the worst thing that ever happened to you change as you thought about it?

Because I was only 13 when I lost my father, for years I thought of his death as the worst thing that ever happened to me. But 22 years later, the production of a play of mine slated to open on Broadway was canceled when the financial backing fell apart. Because by then I had come to terms with the loss of my father, this blow to my career was devastating.

I couldn't write for months. I went into a depression. It took nearly a year to get over it. It made me less trusting of people, especially producers.

On March 10, 1997, my dog, Putney, died. He'd been a part of my life for more than 17 years—four years longer than my father. Was his death the worst thing that ever happened to me? No. But it was one of the most painful things I ever had to get through, and I know I'll feel the loss forever. I also know that, at some point, I'll write about it. How many experiences in your life are really screenplays waiting to happen?

The point of the questions is to see how honest and open you can be *to yourself.*

If you're introspective and self-analytical by nature, my guess is that you'll have an easier time writing down the truth. If you're a "get over it" personality, you might have a harder time recalling things because you've put them behind you.

But since you want to be a writer, dredging up the old pain might turn into a gold mine for you.

The purpose of these exercises is to force you not to play games with your characters. The worst thing any screenwriter can do is write superficial, one-dimensional characters who bear no resemblance to human beings. You've seen movies populated with characters like that. They're tiresome and dull.

Give your protagonist shadings and contours, internal and exterior conflicts. Self-doubt and false confidence are two good ones. Maybe a behavior-altering incident: As a result of someone's pathological lateness, a loved one dies. The death serves as a catalyst to the person being overly conscious about being on time.

And family secrets are always fun. (The gay uncle in Detroit who's 64 and has lived with his "roommate" for the last 38 years. The grandmother everyone pretends is dead but is really in prison for murdering Grandpa and his mistress way back when. The black-sheep brother who is married with four kids but maintains a second family on the other side of town.)

Look into yourself. Then look into the histories of the people you know best. Try to remember all the confidences and secrets you've been told. Then give them to your characters. As you start to develop the protagonist of your screenplay, answer these questions from his or her point of view. It will serve as a solid starting point.

Because you have your screenwriting notebook, no one but you will know how you answered these questions. No one will judge you.

Let's use Question Two as another example. Two people, two different answers.

Person One

The three biggest regrets of my life are that I never learned to ski, I never went to Disneyland, and I never asked Joe Montana for his autograph when I had the chance.

Person Two

The three biggest regrets of my life are that I married a man I didn't love because I was pregnant, I didn't have an abortion, and I didn't get a divorce because he was rich.

One person's answers were fairly superficial, while the other person answered from her heart and soul.

Does it mean that Person One had no profound regrets? Maybe. Maybe not. He could be in denial, hiding his childhood, or protecting himself from some long-ago pain. Or maybe the three regrets he listed are all he's capable of handling. Or maybe he's one of those rare folks who sail through life without anything tragic happening to him, so his regrets would indeed be less complex.

But with both of these people, a character is taking shape. One might have more depth, but the other might be more fun to be around.

The object is to come up with an interesting, appealing character and then to put him or her into an interesting, compelling story.

Through subsequent chapters we'll continue to work on character. Simultaneously we'll work on the story you want to tell. And as we proceed to the next step, I want you to take your answer to Question Four and expand on it.

For example: The worst thing I ever did was have sex with my best friend's fiancée three days before their wedding.

BRIEF EXPANSION

My best friend was the kind of guy who always got the prettiest girls. He fancied himself a ladies' man and liked to brag about all the girls he slept with. But he vowed that the girl he married would be a virgin. When he met Gina, he told me that it was love at first sight and that he was the first guy she'd slept with. I liked Gina and I felt she liked me. I considered her almost like a sister. Three nights before the wedding, I had to drop something off at Gina's house. She invited me in for a drink, and the next thing I knew we were having sex. Afterward she told me that she wanted to get even with my best friend because of all the girls he'd slept with. I never told him what happened. Nine months later, Gina had a baby. That was five years ago. The kid looks like me. My friend and I don't hang out anymore. He told me Gina doesn't like me.

What the expansion does is give more information about the events that led up to "the worst thing" this person ever did and the cause and effect of his action. A story is beginning to blossom. We know something has happened, that there were consequences, and it's easy to see how even more consequences can follow.

After you have completed the expansion of your answer to Question Four, give yourself a pat on the back. You have just written your first storyline.

Doing storylines is a good habit to get into. You force yourself to think ahead.

But because thinking ahead is difficult, storylines are too. I force my students to learn how to do them. Some take to them like fish to water. Others despise them. I like to say that even if you never do one again, it's good to know how to do one because the day might come when a producer asks you for one.

It works like this: You've finished a script and somehow, either through an agent or your own hard work, you've gotten it onto the desk of a producer. It gets read and the producer calls you in and says he likes your screenplay and he likes your writing, but he doesn't want to make your movie.

He asks if you have any other ideas. This is where having a Vague Idea or two comes in handy. Let's say you tell him an idea for a movie. And let's say he likes it. He will ask you for something on paper. One page or two or maybe more. This is where knowing how to construct a storyline and thinking ahead come in handy.

He doesn't want a full-length screenplay or half of the first act. All he wants is that Vague Idea or Basic Premise you pitched him expanded so he can show it to someone else—his partner, an investor, his wife, his mistress, another, higher-ranking, producer, a studio executive, or all of the above.

If you can deliver a solid storyline that gets across the big picture of what the movie will be, you're one step closer to a deal.

Nugget

Circumstances Can Get to
the Best of Us

At your wit's end. At the end of your rope. Backed
into a corner. "I'm mad as Hell and I'm not going
to take it anymore." When mean, rotten, bad, terrible people do horrible things, it's expected. But
when a decent man breaks the laws of God and
man and finds himself in circumstances where
he must go against everything he believes in, the
potential for drama is ripe.

How Did Your Main
Character Get There?

"Every man has a sane spot somewhere."

ROBERT LOUIS STEVENSON

Like most adult males, I've seen my share of XXX-rated movies. Titil-
lation aside, from the first one I saw in a peep-show machine in
Cleveland, Ohio, to the last one I saw on cable TV in the privacy of
my own living room, I've been fascinated with one thing: How do
people decide to have sex for pay and allow themselves to be filmed?

Is it economic? Is it because of a drug problem, which still
makes it economic? Is it to have sex? Is it as the indirect result of a
screwed-up childhood? It's the same with rock stars, the more
flamboyant ones in particular. When did Steven Tyler of Aerosmith
decide to dress that way?

Let's bring it down from porn and rock stars to your uncle
Norm the accountant. How did he get there? With every new person I meet, I'm always fascinated with how he got into the job he
was in. There's always a reason. Your father was a CPA, so it
seemed logical that you would be too.

How did you get your job? How did you meet your mate? How
did you happen to be living where you're living? What lucky break
gave you a leg up on everyone else? What bad break set you back
five years? What did you do that came back to haunt you and
ruined your career?

Does it seem that some people just sail through life, dodging bullets, avoiding tragedies, being lucky, making right choices, always having things go their way?

Knowing how and why your main character got to where he is at the start of your screenplay is important. That's why creating a history, or backstory, for your character can be important.

Like many of the processes discussed, some things work for some and don't for others. I know many people who hate doing character histories, choosing instead to begin writing knowing only a smidgen about the character and learning who he is and what he's all about as they get into the script. I'm like this. Doing character histories filled with minutiae of a person's life doesn't make it easier for me. I prefer to have a general idea of who my protagonist is and what he wants, and get under his skin as I churn out the pages.

I learn when I have my character talk to the other characters. So may you. But I know enough people who won't start writing until they've created a two- or three-page, single-spaced background for a character—and not necessarily even the lead. Actors are known for doing character histories on the characters they play. Acting isn't just memorizing the words. It's understanding what they mean. It's making choices.

If the playwright or screenwriter is around rehearsal, an actor has the option of asking questions about the history of a fictional character. The writer might have answers or might not. Or the answers might not work for the actor. The actor will then begin working on his own character history.

Screenwriters can make choices too: Start writing and discover who your main character is as you go, do a sketchy outline of who he is, or do a painstakingly detailed history.

But whatever your choice, at some point you must ask yourself:

1. Who is this guy?
2. Where has he been?
3. What does he want?
4. Why does he want it?
5. What is he prepared to do to get it?
6. If he gets it, what will happen to him?
7. If he doesn't get it, what will happen to him?
8. What is his greatest flaw? His greatest strength?
9. What does he fear the most?
10. What is his darkest secret?

Like sushi, rattlesnake stew, and steak tartare, you won't know if you like doing character histories until you try one. If it works for you, great. If it doesn't, try a more intuitive approach. Whatever you use should put you on an emotional parity with your character.

Nugget

Uncle Harry's Problem With Gas

What you despise or laugh at in other people you can give to your characters to make them richer, more complicated, and entertaining. Human beings are complex, some more so than others. Human beings have bad habits, eccentric rituals, and obsessive-compulsive behaviors. There's nothing like finding out another person's weak spots, foibles, eccentricities, and good old weird behavior.

Touchy-Feely and Warm and Fuzzy
Versus
Nasty, Bitchy, and Really Evil

"Whoever fights monsters should see to it that in the process he does not become a monster."

FRIEDRICH NIETZSCHE

Normal, happy, well-adjusted people with sunny dispositions and healthy outlooks on life are boring. Not necessarily in real life, but on the screen.

Any actor will tell you it's more fun to play the villain than the good guy. And most actresses would rather sink their teeth into the part of a bitchy, nasty shrew than the All-American girl, super mom, or kindly grandma with an apple pie baking in the oven.

Jack Nicholson's character in *As Good as It Gets* was reprehensible, unlikable, selfish, controlling, obsessive-compulsive, and a dozen other unseemly things as well. We disliked him so much, we couldn't take our eyes off him. If in real life we lived next door to the character he portrayed, we would detest and avoid him and, most certainly, not find him to be intriguing to watch.

But spending two hours with Jack playing Melvin was fun, entertaining, moving, and ultimately satisfying.

Was it Jack Nicholson's Oscar-winning performance that we liked, or was it the part?

With all due respect to Jack, I say it was the part. Dustin Hoffman, Al Pacino, Robin Williams, Robert De Niro, and maybe a dozen other actors could have done things with that role primarily because the writers had created a complex, eccentric, multidimensional character. They could have made him a Caspar Milquetoast type or maybe just a little obsessive-compulsive or Walter Mitty or a mama's boy, but they made him just nasty.

And we loved it.

Just as we loved Nicholson as Bobby Dupea in *Five Easy Pieces*. Not the most lovable guy in the world.

And think of most of the characters Pacino has played. And De Niro. And Sean Penn.

Just as we loved that old curmudgeon of a character called Scrooge.

Not that I'm saying every protagonist has to be obnoxious, repulsive, hateful, or annoying. I can rattle off 25 movies in which the main character was likable and sympathetic and identifiable.

But . . . something was wrong with them. They were nice people, but damaged. Wounded. Screwed up. Like the Julia Roberts and Richard Gere characters in *Pretty Woman*. Meg Ryan played a drunk in *When a Man Loves a Woman*. In *Bulworth*, Warren Beatty played a suicidal politician who had lost his soul. Clint Eastwood played a Secret Service agent haunted by the fact that he hadn't prevented JFK from being killed in Dallas, in *In the Line of Fire*. In *Good Will Hunting*, Matt Damon played an amazingly unlikable Irish punk who happened to be a genius. He was so good and the character written by Damon and Ben Affleck was so dead on that I hated him and wanted him to fail, until he finally saw the light and allowed himself to bend.

The point is, don't make your protagonist sugary sweet, too happy, too content, too unaware, or in denial of his/her problems.

Give your characters something dark that haunts them, maybe not every waking moment, but in the small hours of the night. Give your characters a demon. A weakness. A secret that, if ever revealed, would humiliate them.

Let the warm-and-fuzzy, touchy-feely people stay in your real life (assuming you know any) and keep them out of your screenplays.

Nugget

The Good Bad Guy

Give your hero a worthy opponent. The best James Bond movies have villains who are truly evil but interesting, charming, and strangely likable. And don't be afraid to make him or her truly repugnant. It's more fun that way. If we know our hero will eventually come face-to-face with a wimp or a moderately bad guy, it's boring. But if we know our hero will be facing up to someone who intellectually and physically is his equal, or, even better, his superior, it's just more fun.

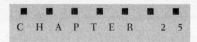

Show Me. Don't Tell Me

"The cruelest lies are often told in silence."

ROBERT LOUIS STEVENSON

Actions speak louder than words. We all heard that for the first time in grade school. It's true in life and it's even more true in the writing of a screenplay.

The point is, if you make a big deal that your lead character is extremely skillful at something—say he's a great salesman or she has the ability to throw together a gourmet meal out of a hodgepodge of random ingredients or he's a coach who knows how to motivate a team with inspirational pep talks—*show* that salesman schmoozing the Hell out of a prospect and *show* that woman putting a fabulous meal together and let's *see* that coach in action.

Not only is it more interesting and will it further the plot, it's a whole lot better than to hear another character remark, "Ya know, that Sally knows how to cook awesome meals out of virtually nothing."

And if a character has a particular skill or ability that will come in handy much later on in the script, show your character utilizing that skill in such a way that we don't know we're being shown something that will have a payoff later. This giving of information is called exposition, and the cousins of exposition are preparation and foreshadowing.

Unlike plays and novels, in which words and time are more readily available to the writer, in screenplays many important moments and points can be made by simply showing a character doing something without having him or anyone else say a single word.

Show me how much you love me, don't tell me. Give me a pay raise, don't tell me how good I am and that I'll be rewarded soon. Don't draw a line in the sand and not take action when someone crosses it.

Actions speak louder than words.

Especially in screenplays.

Nugget

Make It Dirty, Then Clean It Up Until You Can Use It

Don't edit or censor yourself. If your script is running long (Act One ends on page 58, Act Two is 97 pages, and the first draft comes in at 188 pages), don't sweat it. Get it all out. See what you've written. Worry about cutting it down to size later. Same with risqué material. No matter how filthy something is, keep it. Don't stifle yourself. Censor yourself later. There are wonderful gems to be found when you let things happen and don't harness yourself with rules.

That Which Does Not Kill Me
Makes Me Stronger
(and Gives Me Story Ideas)

"If you want to find out if you are lucky, go to a craps game."

GAMBLING MAXIM

I know what it's like to face death. As I touched on earlier, a number of years ago I was robbed at gunpoint in my apartment. A few more details will paint the complete picture.

The only time I ever saw a gun close up was when I stared at the one being pointed in my face. The gun was uppermost in my mind. But if my life depended on it, I couldn't recognize it, nor could I recognize the guy who pointed it at me.

The police who came to investigate asked me if the gun was real. I didn't know. It *looked* real. It never occurred to me that it might not have been real. A toy? No way. It hadn't actually touched me anywhere, so the proverbial sting of cold metal against human flesh wasn't something I experienced.

I tell the story of my mugging less often than I did during the first year and especially the first few weeks after it happened. In those days I spoke of it with an attitude of exuberance and even enthusiasm, almost as if I'd beaten cancer or death, which, in a sense, I felt I had. But inside I was enraged. I played that down.

I only tell the story now in the classroom as an example of the worst thing that ever happened to me. When I tell it now, there is little enthusiasm and even less rage. The telling has become rote for me. I feel like an actor who has played the same role for so long that he can "phone in" his performance. If my audience is receiving the story well, however, I can get into it. If the audience seems dulled or uninterested, I make my points and move on.

After telling the story for more than 15 years, I sometimes find myself questioning my accuracy and wondering if I'm unintentionally embellishing one fact or minimizing something else. I often ask myself if a certain detail is too ironic or quirky or if something sounds too contrived or maybe even too Hollywood.

Did the guy who stuck that gun in my face and held it on me for 35 minutes *really* pet my dog gently on the head? Yes. Did he really pour himself a glass of vodka and then offer me one? Yes. Did I actually have the nerve to ask him not to take my ring because it was a memento from my father? Yes. And after he took a hundred dollars and change from me, did I really have the balls to ask him for a subway token before he left? Yes. His response was, "I'll do better than that," then he tossed a dollar on the ground. (At the time tokens were 75 cents, so this guy was being kind.)

No. There is nothing about that night that is hazy in my mind, starting at the precise moment the incident began: 7:40 P.M. I was meeting friends for dinner at 8 P.M. Being a stickler about arriving on time, I knew from previous visits to their house that it was exactly a 20-minute walk, door to door. So at 20 till eight I walked out of my apartment, locked the door, and there he was.

He was black. Late thirties to early forties. He wore a white winter raincoat. He pulled the gun out of the right pocket of the raincoat and pointed it at my head. I saw him cock the trigger. I remember saying out loud, "Oh God," softly. Inside, I thought, *This is it.*

He asked me if there was anyone in my apartment. I said no, except for my dog. He asked how big the dog was. I told him he was small and, fearing for my dog's safety, made a point of saying that he was extremely friendly.

We went inside. The 35 minutes he was in my apartment seemed like three or four minutes. Never in my life before or since has time sped by so fast. I didn't look at the clock until he left. It was 8:15 P.M. I told him that the only cash I had was in my wallet, that I didn't keep money in the apartment. He told me to hand him the cash and dump my credit cards onto the floor. I wondered why but decided not to ask. I told him I had a savings passbook. He didn't want it. I volunteered that I had a checkbook. My offering him my checkbook resulted in the only light moment in the course of the robbery.

"What are you gonna do," he asked with a gruff laugh and a smirk, "write me a check?"

Besides the money, he ended up taking my wristwatch, a brand-new cassette-tape recorder, and a valuable guitar.

Before he left he dismantled my telephone and took my keys. To my surprise, he said that he would leave them downstairs. I didn't believe that he would. He did. They were on the second-floor landing. The last thing he said to me was that he had a friend waiting downstairs, and if I left the apartment in less than 10 minutes, he would come back and kill me.

Once he was gone, the story becomes anticlimactic. The police came. They made it clear they couldn't do much. The robber wore gloves, so there were no fingerprints. They said I was smart not to panic or fight the guy. A couple of days later I went to a police station to look over mug shots. The person I was convinced was my robber turned out not to be the guy. The man I picked was already in jail. I kept looking at more mug shots, but after about two hours I gave up. Technically, other than the insurance claim, the mugging experience ended when I walked out the door of the precinct house.

But emotionally and psychologically the experience didn't end. To this day I'm far more cautious than anyone I know. Not afraid. Not paranoid. Just cautious.

I was lucky. I had a humane robber. I remember it as if it were yesterday. But I often wonder if he still remembers it the way I do.

I doubt it.

But if there is anything for me to be grateful about in what happened that night, it's that I had a new appreciation for life and, as a writer, it made me experience what it's like to taste death. When I write a character in the jaws of death, I'm not making up the emotions. I've lived it.

This is why experience is such a huge plus for a screenwriter. If you've never experienced something, you might *think* you know what it's like and you might do tons of research to get a *feel* of what it's like and if you have a vivid imagination you might be able to *guess* what it's like. But there's nothing like being in a plane that's nose-diving to the ground and is seconds away from crashing and then doesn't to know what that particular horror (and joy) must be like.

Nugget

The First Five Times You Had Sex

If the first five flights you took almost crashed, odds are you're going to hate to fly. If the first five times you ate sushi gave you food poisoning, there's all likelihood that you won't like raw fish. Oh yes, and if your first five sexual encounters were unpleasant or ugly . . . you see where I'm going. On the other hand, if your first five sexual, flying, and sushi experiences were exhilarating, you're probably going to love doing all three as often as possible. Point is, creating rich, complicated characters means giving them strong reasons for their behavior.

CHAPTER 27

Public Lives, Private Lives,
and Secret Lives

"Everyone is a moon, and has a dark side which he never shows to anybody."

MARK TWAIN

Let's say that the persona we present to our friends, neighbors, and co-workers is our public life and that the person we are at home with our wives, husbands, and children is our private life.

So what's the deal with the secret life?

I personally know of two men who had second families on different sides of the town in which they lived. The family of record with the wife, kids, house, and dog. And the girlfriend with the illegitimate child. Guess who they spent the holidays with.

Then there's the churchgoing, salt-of-the-earth guy next door who works with youth groups, annually donates blood, dresses as a clown for charity, and spends weekends visiting old folks in senior-citizen centers. And did I mention that he has a gorgeous wife and four beautiful kids? Well, he likes to wear his wife's clothes on weekends.

And, of course, there's the super-straight jock who's gay and the girl who dresses like a go-go girl and wears so much makeup you'd think she's a Mary Kay cosmetics saleswoman who radiates sexuality but who's a virgin.

Speaking of virgins, I know of two women well past 50 who have never slept with a man. They're not lesbians. They're not asexual. They're heterosexual virgins. How I know this is not because they told me. It's just information I picked up from people close to them, revealed in confidence by someone who needed to share a bit of surprising information with someone who won't judge but will say, "There's a story in there."

In extremes there are stories. The tale of the 52-year-old virgin is as fascinating to me as the tale of the 32-year-old porn star who finds religion after sleeping with 400 guys. I know of a woman, a virgin until age 45, who finally slept with a guy. One time. And she got pregnant, which was her sole reason for never wanting to have intercourse.

I tell my students to look for the drama in extreme situations. A guy's first day on the job and his last day on the job after 40 years are interesting. Why else are there so many stories about cops either at the end of their career or just starting out? A detective on the job for six years or 14 years or even 23 years isn't as dramatic as the cop who has one week left before retirement and he's never killed anyone and he's put in a situation where he might have to.

That's dramatic.

I have an acquaintance from my youth who is a nun. She went into the convent at the age of 16. I don't know if she ever had a date with a boy. Perhaps she did. She was rather sheltered and overprotected by her parents. Her life experience was, to say the least, limited. I know of another woman who went into the convent after being married and having children. Of these two nuns, which story would be more interesting to watch in a theater?

If you said the latter, we agree. The tale of a woman who has experienced life, marriage, sex, motherhood, child-rearing, and all the problems and complexities that go with the territory would be far more dramatic as she makes a decision to become a nun. Imagine the obstacles. Aren't nuns supposed to be virgins and unwise to the ways of the world?

And human nature being what it is, the nuns who would be training this woman wouldn't necessarily welcome her with open arms. I had 12 years of Catholic education, eight of them being taught by nuns. I remember some of the nuns as pleasant and kind women. I remember a few others as mean-spirited and angry—women who probably didn't want to become nuns but did so to please a parent, women who shouldn't have stayed in the convent but were afraid to leave for one reason or another.

Imagine a few, or even just one, of these angry nuns encountering this woman who became a nun well past middle age who'd experienced marriage and sex and independence.

That's a story.

I think everyone has a secret life, even if it's bingeing on 3 Musketeers bars in the middle of the night when the rest of the family is sleeping, or reinventing oneself in chat rooms on the Internet.

You know what your secret life is. I know what mine is. And I know about the secret lives of a few other people that I found out by accident or gossip or through the person himself.

Odds are that you know about the secret lives of people. This is where you find the shapes and contours of a character. Not in the overt and obvious. But in the dark crevices.

PART 3

Dialogue and Conflict

"You dirty rat."

JAMES CAGNEY

"It is easier to be a lover than a husband for the simple reason that it is more difficult to be witty every day than to say pretty things from time to time."

HONORÉ DE BALZAC

Nobody Can Teach Anybody
How to Write Dialogue

*"Good authors, too, who once wrote better words now only
use four-letter words writing prose. . . . Anything goes!"*

COLE PORTER

I can tell you how to make it funnier, shorter, edgier, longer, tougher, deeper, scarier, smarter, hipper, less formal, and more conversational, but I can't teach you which words the characters will say.

I can assign you a dozen writing exercises in which I give you a dramatic situation, tell you who the characters are and what the objective of the exercise is . . . but I can't teach you which words to use.

I can have a course titled "Writing the Romantic Comedy" in which the goal is to write the next *Notting Hill* or *While You Were Sleeping*.

I can help you plot out a storyline with both romantic and comedic possibilities.

I can show you how to create fully realized, three-dimensional, recognizable human beings with shadings, contours, conflicts, and clear motivations that dictate what they will say and do, but I can't teach you the words that should come out of their mouths.

That's between you and your muse, and if your muse isn't available, you're on your own.

Nugget

Shakespeare Never Murdered Anybody

Neither did Raymond Chandler, Joe Eszterhas, David Mamet, William Goldman, John Huston, Shane Black, Quentin Tarantino, Robert Towne, Billy Wilder, Lawrence Kasdan, or hundreds of other screenwriters who wrote nifty scripts in which the main character killed somebody. So just because you've never murdered anybody doesn't mean you can't write a story about someone who does. And it doesn't mean you can't talk the talk and walk the walk of a killer, even if you're one of those genuinely nice people who don't think bad thoughts or revel in the agony of others or curse or swear or have a low opinion of the human race. If you like to think the best of people, don't let your inherent goodness prevent you from creating a great killer/rapist/kidnapper/ traitor/terrorist or all-around rotten person as your main character.

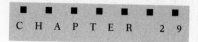

My Friend Robb
Doesn't Believe in UFOs

A UFO crashed in Roswell, New Mexico, in July 1947.

COMMON BELIEF AMONG UFO ENTHUSIASTS

My friend Robb is a skeptic. He doesn't believe in UFOs. I do. I've read every book on the Roswell incident, pro and con. I've pored over the various UFO Web sites on the Internet. The more I absorb, the stronger I believe that we are being visited by extraterrestrials. Robb thinks I'm nuts, or at least naive, or just badly misguided in my search for truth.

We've been disagreeing and arguing about UFOs for years. Whenever I toss out new information, he has something to throw back at me. Robb thinks he's informed because he reads a magazine called *The Skeptical Inquirer*. I think I'm informed because I listen to Art Bell into the wee hours of the night.

Our discussions are never heated, but they are passionate. As strongly as I believe in the paranormal, Robb disbelieves. This kind of dialogue results in low-level conflict. No one will get angry, tempers won't flare, dams of pent-up emotions won't burst. It's just fun, mildly interesting banter.

But if you had a fanatical pro-choicer and an equally fanatical pro-lifer in the same room talking about abortion, you can imagine the sparks that would fly. This dialogue wouldn't qualify as banter. It's more heated. More personal. It gets into one's core belief system.

This is serious conflict. But not serious enough for the parties to come to blows. Or worse. This is the kind of dialogue and conflict that usually starts off with great civility and winds up with the gloves being taken off, but nobody comes out swinging hard enough to draw blood.

Blood gets drawn (and I mean this symbolically) from visceral situations. A husband confronts his wife's lover. A father confronts his daughter's rapist. A woman confronts the man who killed her son in a drunk-driving accident as he comes out of a bar drunk. These encounters represent conflict in the extreme. No one can know how long it will last or how it will end. These are situations that often result in crimes of passion.

You don't intend to strangle the idiot whose carelessness turned your child into a paraplegic, but angry words lead to unguarded conversation that leads to loss of control and either assault, attempted murder, or murder charges being filed.

Conflict is the soul of dialogue. Two lovers kissing and cooing is boring, but if they start screaming at each other in public, it becomes riveting. The nature of what you're writing dictates the level and passion of the conflict. This level is dictated by the personalities involved. Two low-key, reasonable people won't react to the same situation as two high-strung, hot-tempered guys with too much testosterone.

But it's more dramatic when the person you least expect to lose it or get violent does so.

Likewise, the most appealing drama comes when paradox and irony enter into a situation. The white racist male who falls in love with a black woman. The teetotaling moralist, arch conservative who falls for the free-spirited go-go dancer.

My friendly disagreement with my friend Robb is another good example. If I, a true believer in UFOs, see one it's not dramatic. If Robb sees one, it is. If I stumble onto secret government files that prove that every UFO sighting was a hoax, it's dramatic. If Robb stumbled on those same files, all he'd be doing is saying, "I told you so."

The beauty of conflict is that it helps you figure out what characters will and won't say or do in a situation.

A good exercise to see how you handle conflict is to write a five-page scene in which two people who hate each other are stuck in an elevator. Another excellent exercise is to put yourself in that same elevator with the person you hate the most in the world. Five pages. Let it all hang out. You'll be surprised at what you find yourself saying.

Nugget

"Ending" Endings

Your screenplay has answered the Major Dramatic Question. Let's say it's "Will boy overcome all obstacles and get girl?" Your ending's a happy one. He gets her. Sometimes all you need is a fade-out and you're done. Other times you can make an ending more satisfying by including an "ending" ending. Bruce Willis and Kim Basinger made a movie called *Blind Date*, which is about a couple who go on a blind date. He is warned not to get her drunk. Guess what? He gets her drunk and all Hell breaks loose, but despite the fact that she can't drink, he falls for her and in the end they wind up together. Here's the "ending" ending: Cut to Bruce and Kim outdoors lying on a blanket, holding champagne glasses and kissing. We're wondering, *Is he letting her drink, knowing what happens to her?* But as he reaches into the ice bucket, which we haven't seen yet, instead of a bottle of champagne, there's a soft-drink bottle. He reaches for it and refills their glasses. Cute. Sweet. It adds a nice touch to an already happy ending. If you can pull one of these off, do it.

Never Discuss Religion
Or Politics. *Not!*

"Never say more than is necessary."

RICHARD BRINSLEY SHERIDAN

Make sure your characters are at odds, disagreeing, irritating each other, and getting on each other's nerves. Let them be at variance over little things, big things, small points, huge issues.

Just as in life it's fun to push someone's buttons, it's crucial that this happen in your screenplay. If you want to show a couple in conflict, have them fight over where to eat dinner. The woman wants Chinese, the guy wants Mexican. We'll learn volumes about their relationship from this discussion, largely because it won't only be about where they're going to eat.

Talk of a restaurant will invariably lead to one bringing up the other's selfishness, which will lead to one's inflexibility, which will lead to how one is immature, and this will move on to their mutual dislike of each other's friends and in-laws.

As an exercise, write a 10-page scene in which a couple married for seven years argues about where to eat dinner. It can be funny or serious, probably both.

You would never have a 10-page scene in your screenplay, but by writing 10 pages you'll get a lot of good character stuff that you would then edit to make it fit.

On the other hand, you *could* use the entire 10-page scene, provided you break it up. Two people talking for 10 pages in their living room is a lot for a camera to handle. But if it starts in the bedroom, moves to the living room, then goes to their driveway, and winds up in their car, it's no longer a 10-page scene.

PART 4

Finding Your Niche

■ ■ ■ ■ ■ ■ ■ ■ ■ ■ ■

"Consider well what your strength is equal to, and what exceeds your ability."

HORACE

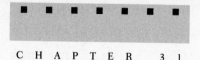

Comedy, Horror, Romance, Mystery, Parody, Action, Drama: Choose Your Genre Wisely

"There is nothing new except what is forgotten."

ATTRIBUTED TO MADEMOISELLE BERTIN,

MILLINER TO MARIE ANTOINETTE

Write whatever you think you can. The problem is deciding what you're best at. If you want to write earnest dramas but all your story ideas sound like nutty comedies and all your serious dialogue is hilarious, you might want to reconsider. I've read plays by people who wanted to be the next Ibsen but discovered they were really the next Neil Simon (not that that's a bad thing).

On the other hand, I've read screenplays by people who set out to write lighthearted romances, but discovered along the way that they were deeper and more serious than they thought.

I believe that most screenwriters are capable of writing any genre of movie. People pigeonholed as comedy writers could write a heartfelt drama, and the rough-and-tumble action writer could churn out a nutty romantic comedy. I've seen numerous adventure films that were hilarious, just as I've seen comedies with moments that were as serious and profound as a play like *Death of a Salesman*, which, by the way, has lots of laughs.

The point is, I think screenwriters should attempt to write for different genres. First of all, it'll be a challenge. Secondly, if you've been writing thrillers and action-adventures with lots of killing, it might be nice to write a small, gentle story, something that might be considered more independent than mainstream.

If you discover that you can write comfortably in a variety of genres, all the better. If you can't handle something different, at least you'll know not to venture too far from the well. This is not to say that every writer can handle every genre ably. The fact is, a few screenwriters can do it all, whereas some writers are better at one genre than another.

Finding the thing you do best is the hard part. There are basically three types of screenplays: mainstream Hollywood, independent, and made for television. But the types of stories are endless. What follows is a listing of genres and examples of each. To present a framework of reference, I've listed three movies for each category.

DRAMA (*Rain Man, One Flew Over the Cuckoo's Nest, Midnight Cowboy*)

FAMILY DRAMA (*Ordinary People, The Subject Was Roses, It's a Wonderful Life*)

COURTROOM DRAMA (*The Rainmaker, The Verdict, Witness for the Prosecution*)

BIO-PIC (*Private Parts, Gandhi, Serpico*)

EARNEST DRAMA (*The Deep End of the Ocean, Searching for Bobby Fischer, Mr. Smith Goes to Washington*)

HISTORICAL DRAMA (*Saving Private Ryan, Glory, Braveheart*)

COMEDY DRAMA (*As Good as It Gets, The Graduate, Some Like It Hot*)

SEX COMEDY (*Mighty Aphrodite, The Tall Blond Man With One Black Shoe, Shampoo*)

CAPER (*Entrapment, The Hot Rock, To Catch a Thief*)

POLITICAL DRAMA/COMEDY (*Bulworth, The Candidate, All the King's Men*)

CHICK FLICKS (*Notting Hill, Thelma & Louise, How to Marry a Millionaire*)

BOYS WITH TOYS (*Armageddon, Con Air, Starship Troopers*)

MEDICAL DRAMA (*At First Sight, The Doctor, Lorenzo's Oil*)

SUSPENSE DRAMA (*A Perfect Murder; Sorry, Wrong Number; Gaslight*)

ROMANTIC DRAMA (*Hope Floats, Living Out Loud, The Apartment*)

ZANY COMEDY (*There's Something About Mary, Airplane!, A Night at the Opera*)

ROMANTIC COMEDY (*You've Got Mail, Sleepless in Seattle, Pretty Woman*)

SCREWBALL COMEDY (*What's Up, Doc?; Bringing Up Baby; It Happened One Night*)

COMEDY ADVENTURE (*Bill & Ted's Excellent Adventure; Honey, I Shrunk the Kids; Ishtar*)

ACTION COMEDY (*Lethal Weapon, parts 1,2,3 & 4*)

BLACK COMEDY (*Happiness, Welcome to the Dollhouse, Heathers*)

FAMILY/CHILDREN'S COMEDY (*Antz, Babe, The Little Mermaid*)

COMING OF AGE (*Stand By Me, My Girl, American Graffiti*)

GANGSTER COMEDY/DRAMA (*Analyze This, Things to Do in Denver When You're Dead, Pulp Fiction*)

ROMANTIC ADVENTURE/COMEDY (*Six Days Seven Nights, Romancing the Stone,* Hope and Crosby's "Road" movies)

PARODY (*Naked Gun* series, Mel Brooks's stuff, early Woody Allen)

PERIOD DRAMA (*The Age of Innocence, Reds, Gone With the Wind*)

THRILLER (*Ransom, Seven, Dirty Harry*)

ACTION THRILLER (*Speed, Die Hard, The Day of the Jackal*)

MEDICAL THRILLER (*Outbreak, Coma, The Andromeda Strain*)

PSYCHOLOGICAL THRILLER (*The Game, The Spanish Prisoner, The Conversation*)

POLITICAL THRILLER (*Arlington Road, The Parallax View, The Manchurian Candidate*)

MYSTERY (*Misery, Frenzy, Ten Little Indians*)

SLASHER/DEAD TEENAGER (*Scream, I Know What You Did Last Summer, Halloween*)

HORROR (*Pet Sematary, Mimic, Poltergeist*)

SUSPENSE THRILLER (*The Siege, Die Hard With a Vengeance, The Omega Man*)

DISASTER DRAMA (*Deep Impact, The Towering Inferno, Earthquake*)

SCI-FI ADVENTURE (*Independence Day, Jurassic Park, Journey to the Center of the Earth*)

There are more. And some of the above might easily be cross-genre—variations on a variation of a variation. It's good to be able to embellish the genre description by saying it's star-driven or character-driven or soft, but it helps to know the kind of screenplay you're writing.

The day will come when you're ready to send it out into the world, and someone will ask you what your screenplay is about. Frankly, before that day comes, you'll find yourself at a party or in a bar or at a lecture when you casually mention that you're writing (or you've completed) a screenplay. Trust me, someone will definitely ask you what it's about. You will sound like a pro if you can rattle off the main storyline in a long sentence or two, pinpoint the genre, and provide the name of an actor, preferably a star or hot up-and-coming actor, who would be perfect for the lead.

Get used to this kind of exchange:

REGULAR PERSON

You're writing a screenplay? Really?

YOU

Yes.

REGULAR PERSON

What's it about?

YOU

It's a coming-of-age comedy called *Sister Sally and Father Bob*. It's about a 15-year-old girl who discovers that her mother is an ex-nun and her father is an ex-priest. A young Claire Danes or Jennifer Love Hewitt would be perfect.

Get comfortable hearing yourself talk about what you've written. The day will come—hopefully, many days will come—when you have the opportunity to pitch your ideas to people in the industry. The more comfortable you are talking about the story you've written, the better you'll be.

Some screenwriters feel comfortable and natural sitting across from strangers or people they barely know, joking, kidding, schmoozing, and being, in essence, salesmen of their own work. But most of the screenwriters I know aren't very good at it. Understand that it's a skill that can be practiced and improved, so do so every chance you get.

PART 5

Screenwriting Tips for Late Bloomers

Including Baby Boomers,
AARP Members, the Viagra Crowd,
and Retirees With a Movie in Them

"I have thought too much to stoop to action."

PHILIPPE AUGUSTE VILLIERS DE L'ISLE-ADAM

Why Being a First-Generation Beatles Fan Can Work to Your Advantage

"Consider what precedes and what follows."

PUBLILIUS SYRUS

You'll never be called the hot *young* screenwriter. Or the gifted *kid* fresh out of UCLA's Screenwriting Program. Or the *girl* wonder who churned out a tearjerker spec script while working weekends at Blockbuster. Or the geeky *teenage* movie nut still on his parents' medical benefits plan who wrote the edgy teen angst thriller that got $450,000 in a fierce studio bidding war.

Hollywood has always put a premium on the proverbial Boy Wonders. Steven Spielberg was directing for television at 21 and had *Jaws* in the can at 27. In the 1920s, Irving Thalberg ran a studio—at 23. Orson Welles starred in, directed, and co-wrote *Citizen Kane* at 24.

Joseph Mankiewicz was in his early twenties and considered a genius back in the '30s. Maybe he was. He went on to write and direct *All About Eve,* among other classics.

Here are some other names you might have heard of.

F. Scott Fitzgerald. In 1939, after his career as a novelist had faltered, he needed money fast. He went to Hollywood and found work as a screenwriter. He was 43 years old.

William Faulkner wrote his first screenplay at 48. Raymond Chandler wrote his first screenplay at 56. He didn't even publish his first novel until he was 51. He wrote the original screenplays for *Double Indemnity* and *Strangers on a Train*. And the aforementioned Joseph Mankiewicz didn't write *All About Eve* until he was well over 35.

Fitzgerald, Faulkner, and Chandler weren't alone.

Screenwriters in the 1930s and '40s came primarily from the ranks of serious novelists, dramatists, journalists, and short-story writers. And most were past 30 when they sank their teeth into this newfangled form of writing, hoping to cash in on the movie business.

Rare was the individual who set out to be a screen "writer." In fact, back in the early days of Hollywood the scripts were called either scenarios or screen "plays."

And unless a screenwriter had aspirations of directing, more often than not he or she still hoped to break out of the movie-writing business and get back to the more respectable and serious work of writing fiction or plays.

But in the 21st century, it's a different scenario.

We live in a culture in which writing the great American novel has been replaced by the desire to write the great American screenplay. Well, maybe not a *great* screenplay, but a script that generates a great deal.

And why shouldn't you be one of the screenwriters who are lucky enough to get one?

WHAT YOU ARE

Fact is, if you were alive when the Beatles came to America in 1964, or if you're closer to 40 than 30 and you want to write a screenplay, you're likely coming to screenwriting with a career or a job or a way of life that you're ready to change.

You've loved movies for as long as you can remember, and now you want to take a shot at writing one. You're probably not sure why you want to try your hand at screenwriting. Maybe it's for the creative experience. Maybe you want to take your shot at the big bucks Hollywood studios are dishing out for spec scripts. Maybe you've succeeded at one career and you're bored and itching to take on a new challenge.

Or maybe you're fed up with how you earn a buck. Maybe you've suppressed a desire to write for 20 years because some hostile teacher intimidated you, but you've finally begun to realize it's now or never.

Maybe there's still a big kid in you who remembers how much you loved going to the movies. How much you have always loved movies. How happy you felt sitting in a darkened theater munching on popcorn and Jujubees. The thrill of going to a flick on a first date, making out in the balcony with one eye on the screen, or getting lost in a film for a few hours when you needed to escape from the real world into somebody else's life. You knew you could always rely on a movie to perk you up, make you laugh, or make you cry.

Or maybe you just want to reinvent yourself for your own private reasons.

Cool. I like people with private reasons for doing things. A 42-year-old journalist took my class because he was disenchanted with the new editorial policy of the paper he worked for. His script was was about—guess what?—a disenchanted journalist. A 35-year-old actress friend started writing to create roles for herself. A multimillionaire Wall Street Master of the Universe in his mid-forties started writing because he was bored with the person he had become. He was rich, powerful, and completely unfulfilled creatively. A 37-year-old high-school choral director started writing because he was burned out.

But make sure you're entering the world of screenwriting, and indirectly, the Hollywood system, for the right reasons. The lyrics to a Rolling Stones song you might've hummed while alphabetizing your eight-tracks in the '70s, might have more resonance to you now: *"You can't always get what you want."*

You're going to write a screenplay with the idea of completing it, then hopefully selling it, then maybe even seeing it get made, but the most important reason you should be writing your script is for the sheer satisfaction of doing so. For creativity, the artist inside you: the screenwriter within.

Whatever is making you decide to try your hand at becoming a screenwriter, you have some very important creative assets, advantages of which Generation-Xers and 20-somethings have few or none at all:

Mileage

Hindsight

Insight

Introspection

Retrospection

Frames of reference

A divorce (or two)

A successful marriage

Loss

Travel

Disillusion

Personal evolution

Therapy

A 12-step program (or two)

Stretch marks
Male-pattern baldness

But mixed in with all these assets and advantages is the Achilles' heel that comes with age.

It's hard for you to put up with things. Simply, you have a lower tolerance for bullshit. Like being in a meeting with someone who falls asleep while you talk to her. If that happened in your present business life you'd be insulted and probably leave the room or point out how rude the person was.

But if it was an upper-echelon producer (or even a bottom feeder who makes only straight-to-video schlock) who dozed off during a crucial pitch meeting, you'd have to ignore it, grit your teeth, and keep on talking.

Could you do that? Could you swallow the comfortable pride you've developed? Could you put that self-esteem you've worked so hard at attaining on the line?

That scenario actually happened to me during a get-acquainted meeting with a producer well into her seventies. She began the session with wide-eyed enthusiasm, but several minutes into it, I noticed that her eyes had closed and she had nodded off.

There tends to be more than one person in the room during a meeting, so after recovering from the shock of this sleeping woman, without missing a beat I turned to her two assistants and continued my pitch pretending, as they did, that she wasn't asleep.

While the same experience can happen to young writers and be just as demeaning for them, this kind of gauche behavior is more difficult to take for the older writer, new or otherwise. You're just not used to having your dignity assaulted without reacting.

Successful salesmen know that making the sale is the ultimate goal. They put up with all their client's nonsense, irrational demands, and BS to get the sale (or until they've had enough and walk away). Screenwriters must have the same philosophy. Unfortunately it's easier to put up with someone's crap when you're young and hungry.

When you're older, you need help. If you're a guy over 40, what would you give for good knees and serious erections? This is where humility, maturity, patience, and savvy enter the picture. If you want the deal, bite the bullet. And if a producer or development executive veers off into humiliation and degradation, bite harder or, like the salesman who has had enough, walk away.

Either way, although your pride might have been assaulted, it will make for a good anecdote. Just like most of the other hurtful/terrible/sad/nasty/dangerous/heartbreaking things that happen to us.

Are you getting the picture?

All the crap you've gone through combined with the joyful high points of your life are worth something to you as a screenwriter and storyteller.

BEEN THERE, DONE THAT, NOW WHAT?

You *really* have been somewhere and done things, unlike fledgling Gen-X screenwriters. Because they're young and still living at home, most haven't done anything real or been anywhere except on a few family vacations. They've watched a lot of movies and TV and have a life vision inspired by that experience.

I don't mean to judge them harshly. That's the world they grew up in—big-screen TVs, satellite dishes, and E! As first-generation Beatles fans and Baby-Boomers, we didn't grow up exposed to the constant media blitz that surrounds us now.

Back in the '60s, there were three TV channels available in major markets—four if you count public television—and the programming wasn't anywhere near the quantity and quality of today. Five if there was a UHF station in your town. There was no such thing as cable, premium channels, video stores, VCRs, malls with ten-plexes, the World Wide Web, or the Internet.

Frankly, I wish there had been. I love all this stuff now. I would have loved it when I was a kid growing up in the '60s.

When someone wants to be a screenwriter or TV writer and his only frame of reference is the world he sees in movies and sitcoms, his lack of life experience shows in the stories he tells and in the characters he creates.

Most are writing from what they've seen rather than from what they've done. So by definition their artistic product is frequently an echo of what's around them. That echo often lacks the visceral feel of real life and real emotions, which is exactly what you have at your fingertips.

You know firsthand about the "slings and arrows of outrageous fortune." All of which is what a writer uses to create vivid and moving stories.

BASIC JOURNALISM 101: NO NEWS IS BAD NEWS

A fundamental of journalism is that a slow news day is bad. Nothing "big" is happening. Slow news translates into soft news—Man Gets Bitten by a Dog. Hard news is when a dog gets bitten by a man and the dog speaks, giving the man a lecture on the fine art of biting.

Understand right now that the talking-dog story is more interesting than the man-gets-bitten-by-dog story. Likewise, know that, from a dramatic point of view, the crap you've gone through is more interesting than the good stuff.

Say you spent a romantic two weeks in Paris with the love of your life. You were treated like royalty, had wonderful meals, met exciting people, and saw French movie stars—*ho hum*. But if your luggage got sent to Madrid by mistake and your wallet was lifted while you were taking a picture of the Arc de Triomphe, and the hotel you thought was a four-star turned out to have only one star and you had to share a bathroom with an old guy named Hans who looked like a Nazi war criminal—*that's* interesting.

It wouldn't annoy your relatives to hear about it while you forced them to watch the slides you took, and it wouldn't bore a movie audience.

Let's try another scenario. A man and his wife are on business in Paris and the guy's wife is kidnapped from their hotel room and he has to find her and his only ally is a trampy French girl who leads him on a wild goose chase and he finds himself attracted to her. And . . .

In case you didn't recognize it, that's the plot of *Frantic*, a 1988 Harrison Ford film directed by Roman Polanski.

To write that movie you had to have been to Paris. The city is a major character. You had to know it inside and out. Reading travel books or interviewing a few people wouldn't be enough. I was offered a rewrite assignment for a movie set in Toronto. The producer called me and said, "Ever been to Toronto?" I said no. He said he needed a writer immediately who knew Toronto. I probably could've called a couple of Canadian friends of mine living in New York, and I could've run to a bookstore or the Internet and done a quick study of the city, but it would've been fake. I didn't get the assignment and, although I could've used the money, a part of me was glad.

To do a solid rewrite on that script would require the same direct experience as the Harrison Ford film. One had to have an understanding of a marriage of two people in their early forties who'd been together a long time and who had problems. To write that movie, you had to know how an adult in an extreme crisis behaves.

Someone in his twenties, unmarried, still living at home, a couch potato, no responsibilities, might very well pattern the Harrison Ford character after his dad. Or worse, a dad he saw in another movie. Or worse yet, a dad he saw on TV.

However, if a writer used his own life experience to capture the emotional depth required of Harrison Ford in *Frantic,* it would be an entirely different—and more honest—interpretation.

Actors do this all the time. They draw on their own experience to develop their roles. It's not just memorizing words, it's getting in touch with what the words mean and finding the nuance and subtlety in them.

This is what you, as someone older starting out in the screenwriting game, can bring to the table.

Nugget

One Thing and One Thing Only

Once you get past subplots, twists, turns, wrinkles, reversals, character histories, and all the other stuff, ultimately a story is about one thing and one thing only: the forward dramatic movement of your main character trying to get what he wants and either succeeding or failing. If he succeeds, the story might continue on further, showing the positive or negative results of getting what he wanted. If he fails, the story might continue on further, showing the positive or negative results of *not* getting what he wanted. Or, if he gets what he set out to get, the story will end—like *The Full Monty*.

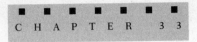

CHAPTER 33

It's What's on the Page,
Not the Age

"A talent is formed in stillness, a character in the world's torrent."

JOHANN WOLFGANG VON GOETHE

If you went to college in the late '60s or '70s (or the '50s), try to remember how many people you knew who wanted to be screenwriters. And how many of them went to a college or university that offered a four-year degree in screenwriting?

Not many, right? And if you went to college in the '80s, the number probably wasn't much higher.

But in the new century it's different. If you're a high-end Baby-Boomer, your child might have his or her sights on a screenwriting career. My guess is that everyone everywhere knows at least one person who is writing a screenplay. In Los Angeles and New York you might know 20.

Because I'm a teacher in one of the acknowledged top-three writing programs in America, most of the people I know are either screenwriters or want to be. And most of these, except for my colleagues, are under 35. Most are under 22. And Hollywood is waiting for them. In some cases, Hollywood doesn't want to wait. Agents and producers are swooping down on kids not old enough to drink. I liken it to professional basketball teams who grab a gifted player directly from high school or after he's played only a year or two of college ball. They lure him with money. He doesn't get a degree or a practical skill. And he's gone.

While the lure of big money and the notion that early success is somehow sweeter is appealing, I know from having taught several hundred students and read more than a thousand scripts that the best writing isn't necessarily coming from the young writers.

This is the mistake Hollywood has been making. It all comes down to what's on the page, not the age of the person who put it there.

BEYOND 20-SOMETHINGS AND GEN-XERS

I haven't spent the last decade in classrooms only with 20-some-things and Gen-Xers. I've lead what one might call a parallel life as a teacher.

Beyond my classes at NYU, since 1989 I've also run a workshop for "older" fledgling screenwriters, with the occasional playwright and television writer. But it's primarily been screenwriters.

When I say "older," I don't mean blue-haired ladies who swooned over Clark Gable or Korean War veterans worrying about their prostates or even 50-somethings torn between cashing in their CDs and moving to a condo in Maui.

I define *older* as people in their thirties and beyond who have had other careers—perhaps successful careers, but they've reached that point in life where they want to go after a dream they've always had: They want to write a movie.

Some of the careers my older students have had include the following:

Psychiatrists (Freudian and Gestalt)
Actors

CPA

Lawyers (criminal and civil)

Graphic designers

TV producers

Insurance agents (life, health, disability)

Computer programmers

Copywriters

A multimillionaire corporate bigwig

Doctors

The wife of a mafioso

Speechwriter

Choral director

High-school English teacher

Art dealer

Secretaries

Voice-over performer

The mother of triplets

Having taught gifted 18-year-olds and mediocre 38-year-olds plus all age levels of talent (or the lack thereof), let me say this right now: Older doesn't necessarily mean better.

Older can often mean tedious, meandering, and pretentious. My experience has shown me that good writing and good story-telling are individual things and have nothing to do with age (or gender or race or religion).

THE BEST COMING-OF-AGE STORIES ARE WRITTEN BY PEOPLE WHO'VE COME OF AGE

I've been paying attention to the Academy Awards ever since they were televised, and I've checked the ages of the winners of the two screenwriting categories: Best Original Screenplay and Best Screenplay From Another Source. The winners under 30 have been damn few. And the winners under 25 are zero.

Most Oscar-winning screenwriters are well into their thirties and up. Golly gosh. I wonder why. Is it because—maybe, just maybe—they've learned a few things about life and the human condition and they've been able to translate that knowledge into intelligent scripts? Young screenwriters just don't have enough in them to deliver the goods.

Except, of course, in 1998.

Good Will Hunting was written by Matt Damon and Ben Affleck, the two stars of the movie. They were both in their mid-twenties. Adding to the fairy-tale aspect of their success (they were struggling actors and wrote the script for themselves), they received more than $500,000 for their screenplay. Good for them. Even after the 50-50 split, taxes, and agent commissions, we're talking serious bucks.

But when I first heard of their good fortune, my immediate reaction was this: If they were two actors in their forties who'd been struggling since their first scene-study course at the American Academy of Dramatic Arts 20 years ago, not only would the script probably not have been made or sold, but the perception would've been that these were two middle-aged losers.

Their age wouldn't have had the sheen of the two young guys, and I don't think they could have gotten their screenplay read, let alone made. There's enough prejudice toward new writers, and it's even worse for older new writers.

Again, this is not to bash the 20-something writers of entertaining, well-written, fun-to-read scripts. Many of the scripts my students at NYU have written are dynamite. And I've seen dozens of entertaining movies written by people under 25 (*Chasing Amy* by Kevin Smith and *The Brothers McMullen* by Edward Burns to name two recent successes).

I have nothing but the best wishes for any writer of any age. Hollywood's preoccupation with youth, however, is a fact that all screenwriters must deal with sooner or later. But despite whatever ageism exists in Hollywood, it doesn't mean you shouldn't try. If a screenplay lands on an agent's or producer's desk and he loves it, he won't suddenly dismiss it when he finds out the author has thinning gray hair, just started menopause, or has two grandchildren. Your script is everything.

So reinvent yourself. You've loved movies all your life. Take a shot at writing one. Make a dent in the system and prove Hollywood wrong.

A Little Hand-Holding

∎ ∎ ∎ ∎ ∎ ∎ ∎ ∎ ∎

"There are moments when everything goes well; don't be frightened, it won't last."

JULES RENARD

TV, VCR, and Membership
in a Video Store

"Rent two, get the third one free!"

VIDEO STORE COME-ON

If you're going to write movies, you have to watch movies. But you have to look at them for more than entertainment. From now on watching movies has to include study, research, and analysis.

I teach a Comedy Writing Workshop. People are required to write an episode of a sitcom currently on the air. I announce that this is the only course they'll take in which they are required to watch TV.

The remark always gets a big laugh. The class thinks I'm kidding, but I'm not. Most of the people taking the course have an interest in becoming comedy writers, but outside of a few shows that they watch regularly for entertainment, they don't really study what they're watching. This is what separates the typical viewer from the person who wants to learn how to write for television.

I urge potential comedy writers to watch as many sitcoms as their dumb-down meters can tolerate. Study the rhythms, beats, number of scenes, number of laughs per scene, length of scenes, and other practical things that I get into in the course of the semester.

The same thing applies to new screenwriters. Watch movies every chance you get. Good ones, bad ones, independents, mainstream, new movies and old, genres you love, genres you hate.

But don't just *watch* them. Discover them. Examine them. Dissect and analyze why some work and some don't. Close scrutiny will reveal why some are great and others are so-whats or never-should-have-beens.

Nugget

Kissing Your Dog on the Mouth . . . or What's Normal to Me Isn't Normal to You

Make a list of five things you do that are perfectly normal to you but make other people think you're nuts. Here's my list: (1) Letting my dog kiss me on the mouth, (2) Having a morbid fascination with old cemeteries and celebrity graves, (3) Eating cereal at night in lieu of a fattening dessert, (4) Buying new clothes and not wearing them for a year, and (5) Going to a movie only in the daytime (and I mean never, never at night) when there aren't many people in the theater because I hate crowds and people talking. This stuff isn't all that weird, but it's not exactly typical. A friend of mine's idea of a snack is to eat cookie dough raw. Another friend's favorite part of a chicken dinner isn't the white or dark meat or a breast or thigh, but the skin. My sister won't eat kidney beans, so when she has chili she picks them out of the bowl. I can't emphasize enough the value of giving characters, main or secondary, nutty little quirks.

CHAPTER   3 5

A Lesson From Chili

"Never use kidney beans."

CHILI PURIST

"Always use kidney beans."

CHILI PURIST

"Chili without meat is best."

VEGETARIAN CHILI PURIST

One of my hobbies is cooking, and one of my best recipes is chili. Chili was also one of the first things I learned to make when the cooking bug bit me.

I started by following my mother's recipe. It was pretty basic: ground meat, kidney beans, an onion, a couple of bacon strips, a can of tomatoes, and some chili powder.

That became my recipe. For a while.

The problem was that I liked my chili spicy. I checked out a few cooking shows on public TV and looked through some cookbooks; one in particular, called *Chili Madness,* contained a diverse selection of chili recipes.

Somewhere along the line I heard about this seasoning called cumin. And somebody else told me about the value of jalapeño peppers. Somewhere else I picked up the idea of throwing in Hershey's cocoa, not for flavoring, but for presentation: It added darkness to the meat. And then came the dash of vinegar. And following that the pinch of sugar.

Then I heard about the theory that dark kidney beans were preferable to light. My aunt Grace liked to use one can of dark and one can of pink for a more artistic presentation.

Along the way I also picked up the thesis that the kidney beans shouldn't be put in the pot until moments before serving. Somebody else used garlic. Somebody else thinks it's sacrilegious to use beans. Somebody else refuses to use ground meat and will use only chunks of beef.

Cilantro can be controversial too. When do you put it in? Too soon and it loses its taste. Too late and it can dominate.

Then it gets crazy. Some people put in a can of beer. Others serve their chili with mashed potatoes. Others still with spaghetti.

The point of all this is the value of feedback and criticism. You write an outline or treatment or first draft and you're alone. Is it good or bad or mediocre or what? Is it worth continuing? Is it too much like something else? Is it a winner?

You talk it out with someone, bounce it off a couple of others. Or you let someone read what you've written.

Although I'm not a believer in brutal criticism, I do believe in honesty. Nobody learns anything from being kind and, well, polite. But I don't believe people learn anything from vitriol either.

The way to benefit from feedback is to be selective in who you show your work to. Just as I learned to be particular about whose ingredients I borrowed for my chili recipe, I've learned to be choosy about whose criticism I accept. My family never sees anything. Ever. They love me and they've always been too kind. Being too kind is almost as bad as being too honest. I've heard criticism given under the guise of being honest that was so brutal it made me sick to my stomach.

I've been able to find a few people who will acknowledge what works and what doesn't work. Hearing what works is fine, but what I'm most interested in is what doesn't. And if I'm really lucky, someone will have suggestions to help fix the problems.

I consider all the feedback and suggestions, accept or reject what feels right, then get to work. It's still my screenplay, even if I utilize the suggestions and feedback or even lines of dialogue.

Just like my recipe for chili: Despite the ingredient suggestions, it's still my chili.

Incidentally, if you're a chili nut: two pounds of ground chuck, two large onions, two cans of dark-red kidney beans (drained and rinsed in cold water) put in three minutes before serving, five cloves of roughly chopped garlic, two cans of whole tomatoes, two jalapeño peppers sliced in half and placed on top, one bay leaf, generous amounts of cumin and chili powder, splash of Worcestershire sauce, splash of vinegar, splash of Hershey's cocoa, well-chopped cilantro two minutes before serving. Cook for two hours.

Serve with beer or margaritas.

Nugget

Feedback and Criticism

Listen to criticism and feedback, but in the end accept and reject what your gut feeling tells you. No critic, teacher, or consultant is 100 percent right. After all, the input and revision take control of the project.

How to Analyze a Movie
in 10 Easy Steps

"In this world second thoughts, it seems, are best."

EURIPIDES

1. Does it get started soon enough?
2. Is what the main character wants clearly established?
3. Are there enough obstacles for the main character?
4. Do we get a sense that the main character has an internal conflict that affects his behavior?
5. Is the character somebody we can root for, even if he isn't especially likable?
6. Are there enough twists and turns so that the story isn't predictable?
7. Do we feel emotionally involved with the plight of the main character?
8. Does the line of dramatic tension intensify as the story moves toward the ending?
9. Is there a change, big or small, in the way the main character now behaves?
10. Is there a satisfying ending (not necessarily happy or dark or sad, but simply satisfying)?

Nugget

Genuine Wit, Scathing Satire, Politically Incorrect Gags, Sex Humor, and Fart Jokes

If you're writing a comedy, make sure it's funny. Let the reader know it's a comedy from the first page. If you can cram in three funny lines or situations on the first page, great. If you can get the reader laughing by the time he turns to the second page, fabulous. If you can make us laugh on every page, terrific. Just keep us laughing. If your intent is to write a nutty, zany comedy in the vein of Mel Brooks, the Farrelly brothers, or the Zucker brothers, make sure it's nutty and zany, not just clever and amusing. Some comedies are witty, some satirical, some irreverent. Whatever kind you're writing, just make sure it's funny. Did I say that you should make sure it's funny? Make sure it's funny.

CHAPTER 37

What Screenplays Will Sell?

"Follow your bliss."

JOSEPH CAMPBELL

I enjoy gambling in casinos. I always go into one full of hope that I'll win a chunk of money. On a good night I'll actually come out ahead and feel great as I leave. On most nights I lose or break even. I'm filled with disappointment as I walk out. But even as I leave I know I'll try again the next night, and the hope I had at the start of the evening begins to grow. By the next evening the disappointment is forgotten and the hope that I'll win a chunk of money has filled me up.

Pursuing a career as a screenwriter is like this: hope and disappointment. You hope your script is terrific. You hope each person who reads it loves it. You hope you get an agent. You hope you get a producer and studio interested in it. You just keep hoping and hoping and hoping. And when nothing has happened on that particular script, you experience disappointment.

Then you do another script and the hoping returns.

This is how it is. Most screenwriters don't sell their first screenplay. Some do, but that happens so rarely that it's not part of the equation. Most screenwriters pay their dues and write a handful of scripts before anything happens. With each script they're filled with hope. And when each one has been passed on enough, the disappointment comes and they start the next.

At the end of the day, being a screenwriter is all about tenacity and patience. You're running in a marathon. How long can you last? Frankly, you can last as long as you choose if you love the creativity and the process of writing screenplays. If it's your bliss, you will find great satisfaction in writing them.

As for getting that first sale . . . it's about luck, timing, connections, right place at the right time, right concept at the right time, God.

And somebody has to like it. Maybe even love it. Somebody with enough access or clout to champion a script through the corridors of Hollywood or even the less crowded hallways of the world of independent films.

When people find out I teach screenwriting, they often ask if any of my former students have succeeded. I say yes. Some have sold scripts and seen their work produced. Others have received paychecks and are in one stage or another of development waiting for it to be made. I take satisfaction in that.

But what gives me real pride is a student who has written a screenplay with interesting, three-dimensional characters and a strong, well-crafted storyline that maintains a dramatic line of tension until the last page.

That's an accomplishment.

Selling it is the reward, and having it made is the icing on the cake.

No one can control what will sell, least of all the writer. I've read mediocre scripts that were bought. I've also read wonderful scripts that were rejected. Students in my classes have written scripts that, were I a producer or the head of a studio, I'd grab in a second. And it's not just my opinion. The other students know when somebody's turned out a winner. So if I praise a script, odds are most of the class is in agreement.

But there's no guarantee that someone who can get it made will like it.

All a screenwriter can control is what he puts on the pages of his screenplay.

"*Life has meaning only in the struggle.*

Triumph or defeat is in the hands of the gods.

So let us celebrate the struggle."

SWAHILI WARRIOR SONG

APPENDIX:
FIVE GREAT BOOKS TO ADD
TO YOUR REFERENCE SHELF

THE WRITER'S JOURNEY: Mythic Structure for Story-tellers and Screenwriters by Christopher Vogler (Michael Wiese Productions, 1998). Inspired by the work of Joseph Campbell, this magnificent book is both a scholarly work and practical guide to utilizing mythic structure and archetypes in the craft of storytelling.

LEW HUNTER'S SCREENWRITING 434 by Lew Hunter (Perigee Books Berkley Publishing, 1995). This is basic training for screenwriters. Lots of great insights and tips direct from the author's screenwriting class at UCLA.

ADVENTURES IN THE SCREEN TRADE by William Goldman (Warner Books, 1989). This long-time upper-echelon screen-writer has written the ultimate insider's book on his illustrious and often maddening career in the trenches of Hollywood.

BIRD BY BIRD: Some Instructions on Writing and Life by Anne Lamott (Pantheon Books, 1994). I read this when I need a lift, when the writing isn't going well or the day-to-day business of living is getting me down. Reading this is a form of therapy for writers. Read two chapters and you'll be refreshed and ready to start again.

WRITE THAT PLAY by Kenneth Thorpe Rowe (Minerva Press, 1939). In my opinion, the greatest book ever written on storytelling and structure. As the title indicates, the book approaches writing from the point of view of a playwright, and the examples are from plays prior to 1940. The wisdom and insights on dialogue, structure, and storytelling, however, are as contemporary as if written today. Unfortunately it's out of print, but you might be able to find it in an old bookstore.

INDEX

ABOUT THE AUTHOR

D. B. Gilles has taught screenwriting, comedy writing, and play-writing since 1988 at New York University's Tisch School of the Arts in the Dramatic Writing Program and Undergraduate Film and Television Department. Many of his students have gotten deals, sold their screenplays, and had their scripts produced. He has written for CBS, NBC, ABC, and Fox and has had deals with the Turman-Foster Company, Carson Productions, Witt-Thomas Productions, Norman Twain Productions, Chris-Rose Productions, and Columbia Tristar, among others. He is the author of 11 plays, most notably *Men's Singles* and *The Girl Who Loved the Beatles,* both published by Dramatists Play Service. He lives in New York City.

D. B. Gilles
Can Be Reached for
Individual Script Consultation
via e-mail at Dbgilles47@aol.com